"Sharon Watkins is one of America's great reconcilers. In my time in the White House, I saw firsthand how Sharon's witness for Christ in the wider world knit both her own denomination and the country closer together, and helped us focus on the issues that matter most. Now, with *Whole,* we have a powerful blueprint for unity that each of us can apply in our own areas of influence. This book is a gift; it will change organizations, and lives."

— Joshua DuBois, Author of *The President's Devotional,* and former head of the White House Office of Faith-based and Neighborhood Partnerships

"There are leaders within the church that everyone should be listening to and engaging. Sharon Watkins—who leads the Christian Church (Disciples of Christ)—is always near the top of my list. Her deep passion for helping Christians live out their faith in ways large and small, the great wisdom she offers from decades of ministry, and the powerful vision she paints of what it means to be one of Christ's disciples in the kind of world we live in—whether or not you belong to her denomination—makes this book a must read. Watkins brings people together, articulates the direction we need, and is one of the best voices we have for bringing faith into public life."

— Jim Wallis, President and Founder of Sojourners

"Come and feast at the banquet prepared for you from the beginning of the world. 'You' means everyone, no exceptions. Turn in here and join the feast, and bring your neighbor with you. Sharon Watkins has prepared a veritable banquet—come and taste—and a tender invitation to come and feast."

— Katharine Jefferts Schori, Presiding Bishop and Primate, The Episcopal Church

"The day I picked up this book to read on a flight made that journey one of my most enjoyable and fruitful recent trips. Sharon Watkins weaves together, in continual vignettes, stories about Jesus, stories about congregations stretching from Enid, Oklahoma, to the Congo, and stories about those who have given hope to others by trying to be faithful disciples. These words are a reminder of who we are, and who God calls us to be as the church. Its poignant examples and insightful wisdom will refresh you, just as Sharon Watkins's ministry continues to do for so many."
— Wes Granberg-Michaelson, Adviser for Ecumenical
    Relationships, General Secretary Emeritus, Reformed Church in
    America

"Here is a powerful expression of how Christians express God's unconditional love to bring wholeness to God's world, not only in good times but in times of disaster, famine, political oppression, and mortal danger. Disciples will especially welcome this account of their own response to Jesus' call, but all readers will be inspired by the way Watkins puts sinewy flesh on an old adage: 'God did not tell the world to go to church, but God did tell the church to go into the world!'"
— Jim Winkler, General Secretary and President, National
    Council of Churches

"In this engaging primer on the Christian life, Sharon Watkins shares stories that reveal the myriad ways we encounter God in our lives. She shows how discipleship, solidarity, and radical love are the new watchwords not just for ecumenism but for all authentic Christian witness today."

— Olav Fykse Tveit, General Secretary, World Council of Churches

"It's a different kind of book than I expected. I thought it would be a scholarly presentation on the meaning and content of the 'identity statement' of the Christian Church (Disciples of Christ). But what I encountered was a book that begins and ends with personal stories and vignettes centered upon the key concepts that give us our identity as a faith community. And from those stories, I found myself being invited to reflect upon my own experiences around the Table, being welcomed, and finding wholeness and unity. The power of this book is not so much in its teaching, but in its invitation to share our stories of faith!"

— Robert Welsh, President, Council on Christian Unity

WHOLE:
A CALL TO UNITY IN OUR FRAGMENTED WORLD

SHARON WATKINS

CHALICE
PRESS

ST. LOUIS, MISSOURI

www.chalicepress.com

Print: 9780827243132   EPUB: 9780827243149   EPDF: 9780827243156

Library of Congress Cataloging in Publication data available upon request

Printed in the United States of America

For my church,
seeking wholeness for the sake
of a fragmented world.

CONTENTS

Acknowledgments

There are so many to thank…

Glenn Carson and Brad Lyons for encouraging this project in the first place, and Pablo Jimenez for the huge task of editing.

Several people have read and given extensive input to earlier drafts—Cathy Myers Wirt, Cherilyn Williams, and Robert Welsh. Rick Lowery and Keith Watkins have read every word and tried to help improve the outcome. Beth Sullivan has given invaluable help tracking down footnotes and handling matters in the office while I've been writing.

Others have read early portions and offered encouragement and insight: Charisse Gillet, Samuel Ramirez, Paul Tshe, Kris Culp.

If I could channel all their wisdom, this would truly be a magnificent work.

As it is, this is my book—containing my vision of church. It is not intended to be a last word, but simply my input as we followers of Christ try to find our way forward in this early twenty-first century as a movement for wholeness. I offer these reflections as part of an on-going conversation among Disciples and beyond. I offer them in gratitude to a church that has nurtured me and been home to me throughout my life.

Not everyone—certainly not all Disciples—will agree with all that I have said here. Some will take issue with particular examples I have given. I hope that will not take away from the broader message. Disagreement as an integral part of diversity does not have to be disagreeable. Differing points of view do not belie the foundational gift of wholeness that is God's gift in Jesus Christ. In fact, diversity, and even disagreement, serve to render more profound the faith-claim that in Christ we truly are one. The invitation here is to make the decision to love each other as God loves us and to let our love for each other be our message of hope to a fragmented world.

Speaking of love…

The love that surrounded me as a child and still emanates today from my parents, Keith and Billie Watkins, first helped me to name God as love.

The unspeakable joy that comes from being mother to Bethany and Chris takes the meaning of love to a deeper level than I ever could have imagined before they came into my life.

And Rick—my partner in life and ministry for over thirty years—it would take a much better exegete than I will ever be to know where your thoughts end and mine begin. Our lives are hopelessly intertwined. What I have learned from you of love gives me the confidence that what I say is true.

Sharon Watkins

Introduction

*We are Disciples of Christ, a movement for wholeness
In a fragmented world.
As part of the One Body of Christ,
We welcome all to the Lord's Table as God has welcomed us.*
~Disciples of Christ Identity Statement~

When the President of the United States asks a favor, it's hard to say no.

The phone call came during a silent retreat. But seeing the number, from Washington, D.C., I went ahead and answered. It was an invitation—a surprising one—asking me to preach at the National Prayer Service on the day following the inauguration of the President.

It would be a Christian service with interfaith sensitivities, I was told. The congregation would consist of "the nation," with all its diversity. And I would be the first woman ever to preach at this service, which had a tradition going back to the inauguration of George Washington.

I tried to treat the assignment like any other sermon, steeping myself in prayer and scripture. In this case, I also dwelled in the hymnody and patriotic songs of our nation. But really, what is the source of common authority for a congregation of every faith and no faith? What is the appropriate religious word for a civic occasion? And who am I to preach to the President? (Not mention the Cabinet,

1

the Congress, the Supreme Court, and half of the religious leaders in Washington!)

On the day of the service, it did not feel like "any other" sermon. My husband and I boarded a special bus early with other participants in the service, some of them almost as famous as the President himself. At the National Cathedral we went through metal detectors. Colleagues said they were lifting me in prayer. I responded to one, "That's good, because this is too big for me."

We waited a long time while the many worshipers arrived and went through security. Time enough for nerves to fray, palms to sweat, breath to shorten.

Eventually the moment came to line up for the opening procession. We started walking into the back of the Cathedral toward the aisle. My knees were quaking just a little…

The architecture of a cathedral intends to draw the eye upward. The vast height and the curve of the arches all speak of the transcendence of God. My eyes lifted to the top of the sanctuary walls. Magnificent colors of stained glass shone next to fainter colors projected there by the brilliance of the morning sun streaming through the windows on the opposite side. The prelude music swelled toward its transition to the processional hymn. I took a deep breath.

And then…

I had a physical sensation as if some force of nature had breathed in, gently drawing out of me all that was nervous and anxious. I literally felt it all flow away from me up toward the heights of the cathedral, seemingly pulled by a gentle but insistent Spirit. I remembered: We are here to worship! God is in this place.

In that cathedral, designed to awe worshipers by the transcendence of God, I felt instead the gentle presence of God as close to me as my very breath, accompanying me in that moment as in every moment of my life. I whispered a prayer of gratitude and stepped forward to preach.

In one sense, a prayer had landed me in this situation in the first place. In early summer 2008, Senator Barack Obama had just wrapped up his party's nomination for president. His staff invited forty or fifty Christian leaders to spend an afternoon in conversation with the candidate. They asked me to offer the closing prayer.

Over the course of those few hours, the conversation covered topics of profound disagreement among those present. At times the tone of the conversation grew tense as persons spoke from the heart and challenged the assumptions and assertions of other speakers.

In closing, we gathered around the senator to lay hands on him and ask that the Spirit of God be with him, his campaign, and with all of us in the weeks ahead. Praying, we turned away from our differences and faced together toward God's presence and love. The sense of the room stilled and calmed into a feeling of blessing.

Months later, I am told, when it came time to select the preacher for the national prayer service marking President Obama's inauguration, the staff remembered that time of prayer earlier in the summer. Hoping also to add to the history of the weekend by calling a woman to preach at the inaugural prayer service, they invited me.

—————— —————— ——————

It was not my first time to stand as the "first woman." In July 2005 also, my knees were quaking but my spirit steady as I prepared for installation as the General Minister and President (GMP) of the Christian Church (Disciples of Christ), the first woman to serve in this role as leader of my denomination.

I knew that I had a big job on my hands. My first move was to invite other Disciples to pray with me daily for the mission of the church. Ten thousand people signed up to be daily prayer partners through "10,000 Disciples Praying" (affectionately known in our office as 10kDP).

With the intercessors hard at work, the next call went out to a group of people who could help the Church begin thinking about where we found ourselves at that precise moment and where God might be calling us next. This "visioning" process involved people from across the life of the Church and was chaired by the Rev. Dr. Cynthia Hale, founding pastor of Ray of Hope Christian Church in Atlanta.[1]

Perhaps the best thing that came out of our visioning was a new identity statement. As a church, under the leadership of General Minister and President Richard Hamm,[2] we had already answered the question, "What are we to do?" with a mission statement incorporated into a document called the "2020 Vision."

Our mission
Is to be and to share the Good News of Jesus Christ,
Witnessing, loving and serving,
From our doorsteps to the ends of the earth.

We had also described our vision:

To be a growing, faithful church marked by
True community, deep spirituality and a passion for justice.

But the 21st Century Vision Team felt strongly that there was a prior question to answer. That question was, Who are we? Why is there a Christian Church (Disciples of Christ) at all? Within the whole family of God, what is our particular Disciples identity?

As we shared our understanding of our own history and way of being, we remembered that, at our core, the Christian Church (Disciples of Christ) emerged as a Christian unity movement. Historically, we held that a united church would offer a contagious witness to the world. It would, in effect, "sell itself" by its visible witness of love. The particular embodiment of that unity vision changes with the cultural and historical context. Yet always at our heart has been the conviction that all are welcomed among Disciples. We celebrate lay leadership. We do not bar anyone from the communion table. "Unity is our Polar Star," we say, and we know that radical diversity is what makes unity in Christ mean something. Our vision team's quest for the identity markers that precede vision and mission had led us to our core historical value of unity for the sake of the world.

We discovered, much to our distress, however, that in our time many Disciples could no longer articulate our core value of unity. The term "unity" itself had lost luster through its association with the specific and now dated unity efforts of previous generations. We looked for a way to state our conviction that would work for twenty-first–century Christians. We arrived, finally, at a succinct statement that has been embraced by Disciples across the United States and Canada.

We are Disciples of Christ, a movement for wholeness in a fragmented world. As part of the one body of Christ, we welcome all to the Lord's Table as God has welcomed us.[3]

⸺⟨⟩⸺ ⸺⟨⟩⸺ ⸺⟨⟩⸺

In the inaugural sermon, I had fifteen minutes to make my point. I wanted to say something authentically Christian, but also to communicate beyond a Christian audience to society at large. I chose as the key text for my sermon a biblical passage in which Jesus sums up his message in one word: *love*. I reminded my listeners that what we nurture in life, good or bad, will grow and flourish. In the end, Christians, Jews, Muslims, and others in the audience told me it had been an important word.

Given that, in many ways, this experience inspired me to write this volume, I have included the full manuscript of the Inaugural Sermon, titled "Harmonies of Liberty," as an appendix to this work. In the following chapters, I will expand on those fifteen minutes and further reflect on Jesus' call to his followers to love God and neighbor.

The key words of our Disciples identity statement present the jumping off point for my thoughts. Vignettes from my own experience within the Christian Church (Disciples of Christ) will help sketch what these words mean to me, as well as indicate what the identity statement tries to capture for Disciples and others in this twenty-first–century world. Rather than providing a thick description or comprehensive theological discourse, this collection of stories and reflections serves to point in a general direction. In order to follow the chronology of my own faith experience, I will start at the end of the statement and move toward the beginning: *table, welcome, wholeness, movement,* and *Disciples of Christ.*

I write in part for the Disciples Church itself, to help pull the meaning of our identity statement out from the inarticulate muscle memory of our community that causes us to act in particular ways without always knowing quite why. I argue that we are a community of faith that makes particular sense for the twenty-first century—a church whose time has come—with a message and a way of being that can work for this time. I also point out that, for the message to resonate fully, we need to clean up our act.

I write in part to non-Disciples to introduce a branch of the Christian family that is not as well known as some others.

And I write for anyone who might be interested in a way of being in the world that involves deep spirituality, true community, and a passion for justice for the sake of the world and its future. I write for those seeking hope that humanity can live together with our diversity as a cherished gift. In a word, I write for those seeking *wholeness*.

This book grows out of my experience and reflection as a lifelong member of the Christian Church (Disciples of Christ), as an ordained minister for thirty years, and as General Minister and President in the middle of my second six-year term of office.

⸺♦⸺ ⸺♦⸺ ⸺♦⸺

In many ways, 2005, the year of my first election as GMP, seems like another era. Our world is changing so rapidly that from one year to the next we can find ourselves facing challenges of a whole new variety. In the church we may feel like Abram and Sarai in the Bible; in Genesis 12, they started out at the call of God with no roadmap, no GPS, no known destination. We, too, are confronting issues different than any of our predecessors could have imagined. For an institution like the Church, responding to such rapid change can be daunting.

In the end, particular institutional forms can change. What really matters for followers of Christ is the relationship with a living, loving God, a God who calls us to love each other, to create communities of care and equipping for wholeness, so that the love and hope we know through our relationship with Christ can truly be carried from our doorsteps to the ends of the earth.

Sharon E. Watkins
Indianapolis, Indiana
January, 2014

1

Table

As God Has Welcomed Us

Dense African forest pressed into the nearly impassable road. The drivers maneuvered carefully. Even so, the van and pick-up seemed to bump and slide forward, rather than actually roll along the muddy ruts. We Americans were grateful that our Congolese hosts had been this way before.

Rounding a bend, the "nearly impassable" route became totally blocked. A large tree had fallen, stretching from one side to the other. We all piled out of the vehicles and stood there…scratching our heads.

A rustle in the brush alerted me to a group of village children gathering—curious, as children will be. Their moms were with them. The women carried parcels wrapped in brightly patterned cloths. In a moment, some men followed, with machetes and knives in hand. Four other men were hauling a door, a big, wooden door.

The men with the tools went straight to the tree and got to work, cutting and tugging. The others placed that door on the forest floor, and the door became a table. The women began unwrapping their bundles to reveal peanuts and bananas and Orange Fanta! (Where did they get the Fanta?)

They spread that feast and invited us to partake.

We were strangers on the side of the road. People of that place came out to us and met us in our need. They spread a table, and we felt welcome.

There is something about being invited to the table...

Where Food—and More—Is Shared

As places to eat, tables matter.

Our first "tables" come to us: Mama's lap, a bouncy-seat on the floor, a high chair. Family life often takes its most representative shape at table. During my childhood, the family table was black Formica, squeezed into the kitchen breakfast nook. My siblings and I joined our parents there for dinner at six o'clock sharp every evening. My own children were not blessed with such regularity. For them the family table sometimes consisted of fast food in the back seat of the car on the way to dance class or football practice; or, too often, a late meal gobbled down in front of the TV while Mom and Dad prepared for meetings. In both family styles, however, the table represents a most basic need: where food is shared.

Tables also exist as more than places to eat. Tables can represent gathering in community. At the "table" in the Congolese forest, we accepted the food as symbolic more than fully nutritional. The villagers were meeting our immediate needs. They offered comfort, hospitality, and a solution to our transportation problem.

The experience by the side of the road in Congo should not have surprised me. Working in Congo, I had already experienced the generosity of Congolese hospitality. In particular, Mama Kisita befriended me. Not much older than I, Kisita was married and had two children—with a third on the way. Based on the location of her home, the screenless, glassless windows, and the spigot out front of the house for water, we would have called her family "poor." Yet, whenever I stopped by, she unobtrusively pressed a coin into her young son's hand and sent him off somewhere. He soon returned with a Coke, which she poured and set before me along with some peanuts. Every time I entered her home, she welcomed me "at table" with her. She probably went without, in order to make that welcome happen.

Mary Roach, author of *Packing for Mars*, in a National Public Radio interview describes the gathering role of tables.[1] Her book tells

Table 9

more than you'd ever want to know about the challenges of space travel—including quite a bit about eating in space.

In zero gravity the littlest thing—such as an escaping crumb, for example—becomes a problem. Until you can contain it, that crumb floats, threatening to show up and distract you at any given moment. A lot of food in space, therefore, is delivered from a tube directly into the mouth. No spoon or fork required.

You miss much eating that way: the smell, the presentation—the crumbs. But it turns out that what you miss most is the social part, the conversation, the sharing around a table.

So now, long duration space ships are fitted with a completely nonfunctional table—nonfunctional, that is, for sitting down to eat in zero gravity. The table is completely functional, however, as a center for gathering, for being together, for establishing community. Even when the food is more or less symbolic in nature, the gathering at table matters for the sense of community it creates.

Another trip, another table.

My two companions and I pulled into the hot, dusty town of Scottsbluff, pedaling bicycles. We'd finally crossed into Nebraska after several days of hard riding through a Wyoming heat wave. The long day would end as soon as we found a place to stay.

We made a phone call to First Christian Church (Disciples of Christ). "We're Disciples traveling through on bikes," we said. "Can we sleep on your church floor?" Sometimes this kind of call resulted in nights on couches in a church parlor and a place to cook a hot meal. Tonight would be different. We would sleep in real beds, guests of church members.

After wonderful, steamy showers, we thought our day had reached its zenith. We truly hit the bonanza when our hosts loaded us into their vehicles and drove us to dinner. At the park outside of town, we joined others from the church in a potluck picnic and cookout. The smell of grilling burgers and hot dogs promised a great summer meal. Wooden tables were loaded with salads and desserts, which for once (given the bike riding) I could contemplate with great anticipation.

My strongest memory of that evening was after the meal, sitting around the fire pit. Our hosts talked of church doings. We cyclists recounted adventures on two wheels. Someone offered a spiritual reflection. All of us sang together. I had never before set foot in Scottsbluff, Nebraska, but sharing table and stories with these people I felt the embrace of community.

Both the Congo forest table and Scottsbluff picnic table bore food: of physical importance. Both tables were the center of a welcoming community: of social and emotional importance. Scottsbluff was particularly satisfying, because these good church people provided for us, as well, a renewing spiritual oasis on our journey. Embedded within the welcome of First Christian Church, Scottsbluff, I experienced the welcome of God.

God

How did my mind travel from a Nebraska campfire to the welcome of God?

Not everyone believes there is a God. And yet, for most of history, human beings have seemed to be aware that something exists before us and beyond us. Petroglyphs on ancient rocks, prehistoric burial practices, sacred writings through the ages—all point to humans perceiving a presence that transcends our own senses. Whether it is called a force, a spirit, or a being, this transcendence—God— exists beyond human seeing, yet always within human longing. The constant emergence of religion gives shapes to that longing.

⸻◦∞◦⸻ ⸻◦∞◦⸻ ⸻◦∞◦⸻

One day a woman stopped at the church building where I was pastor. I didn't know her. She was young and seemed nervous to be talking to a stranger, and a minister at that! She had this feeling the church might have something she needed, she said. "To be honest," she continued, "the church has always frightened me. I've never actually been in one before… The cross, on top of everything, just seems kind of creepy."

Not a very promising start to a conversation!

I couldn't really blame her. Christians "as seen on TV" are not always particularly attractive. In spite of those with good intentions, "electronic religion" has been plagued with too many ministers

Table 11

with a public morality but secret lives of sexual misconduct and unfaithfulness, Christian judgmental attitudes about personal matters, and an anti-scientific perspective often branded as "Christian."

Surveys tell us my visitor is not alone in her discomfort with Christianity. According to Jon Meacham of *Newsweek*,[2] in the twenty-first century people in the United States are becoming increasingly distanced from the church. Today people in North America and Europe are less likely than ever to self-identify as part of any organized religion. The world's Christian center has moved from Europe and North America to the Southern Hemisphere.[3] Yet, spiritual longing continues to exist in the north. Surveys tell us that people in the United States make a distinction between "spiritual" and "religious." Many people may not claim a particular "religion," but they do continue to believe in God. They pray. They continue to have an interest in the "spiritual life."[4]

The young woman in my office had instinctively come to a church to work out her spiritual questions. She seemed to be an example of a "spiritual but not religious" person trying to find her way to God. For two millennia, many people have gotten to know God by getting to know Jesus and his followers. The God I wanted to introduce her to is a God of love who I have gotten to know through stories and experiences of Jesus Christ, through my involvement in the church. I wanted her to know the God who would be present in a Nebraska church picnic, or by the side of the road in a tropical rain forest, or in a Congolese woman's home, or with a lonely American woman seeking a spiritual center.

To know this God, we begin with Jesus.

———

Jesus started out as a first-century itinerant Jewish teacher in a world ruled by the Roman Empire. In his teaching, he described a contrasting world in which all people and communities were well and whole, strong and free. He first caught public attention by healing physical and mental illness. Word began to spread that, with his touch, lame people stood up and walked, blind people could see, and lepers were cured of their infection and liberated from the quarantine that was part of this terrible illness. The crowds gathered in hopes of physical healing, but Jesus offered more than individual wellness. He extended community wholeness as well. Most amazing of all, his vision included everyone.

One day word was spreading that Jesus would pass through a particular town. A citizen of that town, a tax collector named Zacchaeus,[5] decided to get a look at this healer. He made his way to the road where Jesus would pass. Not very tall himself, and the crowds being large, Zacchaeus climbed up into a tree in order to see.

Just as Jesus passed the tree, he glanced up and noticed Zacchaeus sitting there. As if it had all been planned, he called out, "Come down from there! I want to eat at your house today." Over that meal, in conversation with Jesus, Zacchaeus caught a different vision of how life could be. He vowed to give up the cheating and overcharging that had been his standard practice. He promised to repay, many times over, anyone he had wronged.

Zacchaeus' touching story did not meet with everyone's approval. Some who heard it began asking the question that would turn into a frequently repeated refrain: Why does that Jesus eat with sinners? Once again the significance of the table went beyond the food that was consumed there. It was also about the community that gathered around that table.

It was a logical, if self-righteous, question. Jesus didn't stop with inviting himself over to one particular tax collector's house on one specific day. On many occasions, he made a point of sitting at table, eating and being in community, with tax collectors and sinners.[6] In a time when it was socially unacceptable for men and women to mix socially at all, he shocked friends and strangers alike by talking to women right out in public.[7] He welcomed children,[8] with their runny noses and noisy play, to join the circle of his hospitality. His own closest disciples included some unsavory characters: another tax collector and a revolutionary,[9] to name two.

For those who hung around and paid attention, it began to make sense. A common theme was emerging in Jesus' actions and his teaching and his welcoming table. That theme was love.

A God of Love

A little church in Colorado was growing. At a point when all reason said they must soon shut their doors due to low attendance and inadequate financial support, they had switched gears. Instead

Table   13

of hunkering down to protect what little they had left, they had thrown wide open the door. In particular they offered hospitality to Twelve Step Groups.[10] The people of the church believed they were acting in the tradition of Jesus' life and teaching, offering shelter to neighbors, setting tables of care. People struggling with addictions of various sorts found a nonjudgmental, welcoming oasis in that church building. Soon people from the groups and their families started wondering about this church. Who were these people who had extended to them a helping hand? The church began to grow in numbers again and get back on its feet financially. Best of all, they were now able to expand their ministries of hospitality and care further than ever before.

One day the minister was downtown and overheard his congregation mentioned with scorn. "Oh, yes. That's the church that will take anyone." When he reported back to his congregation, they received the description with pride. "We're the church—in the name of Jesus—that will take anyone!" They put it on their sign out front as the church motto! This congregation had caught on about love.

In the English language, the word *love* can take many shades of meaning. Greeting cards evoke a sentimental "love." Movies often propose stronger stuff: the "love" of friendship and the "love" of erotic desire. In some languages, there are different words for these two different kinds of love. In the original Greek of the Christian New Testament, each of those kinds of "love" is represented by its own word: *philia* and *eros*. English speakers add an adjective to make the distinction: romantic love, brotherly love, erotic love.

For Christians, the word *love* takes on yet another meaning. The biblical Greek language calls it *agape*. Agape is "spiritual" love,[11] a self-giving love. It is the essence of altruism. Agape puts the other person first.

Jesus gave an example of agape love in one of his most famous stories, often called the story of the good Samaritan.

A man sets out on a journey alone, on a road known to be the haunt of thieves.[12] Sure enough, he is attacked, robbed, and left for dead. Two different people, religious authorities of his own nationality, pass by and do not stop to help. A third person approaches. He is of a despised ethnicity. Normally there would have been "no love lost" between the stranger and the wounded man. Yet this third passerby stops, bandages the injured man's wounds, and takes him to an inn. The stranger, known only as "the Samaritan," even gives money out of his own pocket to be sure the injured man has a bed until he heals.

This, says Jesus, is what it means to show love. You love your neighbor as yourself. You become a neighbor by showing mercy to the one who needs it.

Jesus lived his life demonstrating this kind of love. Not a mushy sentimentalism, but rather a willing decision to care for the well being of the other as much as he cared for himself. He approached people with a listening ear rather than a judging mind. He brought physical healing with a touch. His words offered forgiveness and emotional wholeness. He shared meals with the outcast and interacted with the contagious. He honored those whom society shamed, and he urged the powerful to be gentle and merciful. He knew that his nonviolent resistance to the ways of the world and of the Roman Empire brought great risk to himself. Even so, he believed that this kind of love was of God. And he believed so strongly in the power of God's love to prevail that he continued to press forward. He urged his followers to do the same. God has it in mind for humans to live this way, he said.

Which brings us back to God. Jesus was not just making this stuff up. He was trying to live in a way that would show the world what God is like. The God he experienced was a God of self-giving love who also knows something about the welcoming table.

———※⁂※——— ———※⁂※——— ———※⁂※———

Jesus cast his ministry in the tradition of Hebrew Scripture, the tradition of his own birth. The biblical author Luke tells that Jesus began his public ministry with a kind of "inaugural address." On that day, Jesus sat as a teacher would, and read straight out of the prophetic tradition. "The Spirit of the Lord is upon me, / because he has anointed me / to bring good news to the poor. / ...to proclaim release to the captives / and recovery of sight to the blind..."[13] The people listening recognized the ancient voice of Isaiah. The rallying cries of other prophets from previous generations echoed in their

Table 15

memories as well. The worshipers were familiar with prophetic scriptures being read, calling on the people to treat workers fairly, to make sure that the vulnerable widows and orphans and sojourners were cared for.[14]

They remembered biblical stories in which God interacted with their forebears, offering and receiving table hospitality. Abraham, the father of the nation, might have come to mind...

One day Abraham[15] looked up from his doorstep—actually from the flap of the tent, which was his home, and saw three strangers approaching. Abraham was head of household; he acted automatically to protect. As dictated by his culture, he went out to meet the strangers and invited them to the table.

The social code of this Middle Eastern desert people required that if a stranger passed through, people of the place offered hospitality. The ethical duty of hospitality protected home and family. Travelers in the desert encountered intense heat, thirst, animals, and thieves. In such harsh conditions, strangers might not be able to meet their own needs and could become dangerous to established households along the way. When households extended hospitality, they lessened the desperation of the vulnerable stranger and thereby protected the family.

So, as the strangers approached, Abraham walked away from his family tent toward them with an offer of water, a place to rest in the shade, and a hot, home-cooked meal. He knew that if they accepted his offer all would be well. And so it was. Not only did the strangers take him up on his offer, they extended a blessing in return. Revealing themselves now as messengers from God, they made an astonishing prediction. They announced that Sarah, Abraham's wife, long infertile, would give birth to a son in the coming months... Could even God do this? It was now years after all hope of such a possibility had past. The visitors' announcement was good for a laugh, at least, and Sarah did laugh.

In retrospect, Abraham and Sarah took a more thoughtful view. She became pregnant after all. It was now perfectly clear that in those strangers, God's own messengers were present at their table. Sarah and Abraham came to understand God as one who cared enough about human affairs to adopt this obscure family in their generational vulnerability and to bless them with descendants as numerous as the stars. Abraham had issued a socially required invitation, but they shared much more than food at the table that day. Through the hospitality they offered, Abraham and Sarah were blessed with the presence and care of God.

When Jesus read from the prophet Isaiah at the beginning of his ministry, this story passed through the minds of the people in a flash. They knew the rest of the story: that God stayed faithful to Abraham and Sarah's descendants through the ages. In the Bible, generations later, their children had grown into a nation.[16] At a certain moment their circumstances had taken a devastating downturn, and they had ended up as slaves in Egypt. Then in the hour of their greatest need, God had intervened again, this time to set them free.

Their journey to freedom had involved more than forty years of circuitous travel. It also had given them the opportunity to get reacquainted with this God who had freed them. One of the important tales from that desert journey was about how God had fed them.[17] Nearing starvation in the cruel wilderness, they had awakened one morning to find a kind of frost on the ground. It turned out that the frost was bread, just the right amount for each family to gather for the day. This "manna," as they called it, appeared day after day. God spread a simple "table" in the wilderness to meet their most pressing needs.

Jesus intended for his ministry to remind the people of their long history with God. God had stepped into the life of a vulnerable family with no generational future and given them a future. God liberated slaves and welcomed them at table. The particular reading Jesus chose in the synagogue that day pointed out that God expects those in the divine circle to treat others with similar care and concern. Jesus' ministry set out to expand that circle by reacquainting people with God.

Jesus' teaching painted a picture of a powerful and benevolent, loving God, more like a caring parent than an awesome ruler of the universe. In fact, Jesus' favorite name for God was "Abba," a child's affectionate name for a father.

In one beloved story, Jesus spoke of one father and his two sons.[18] The older son, like the stereotypical firstborn, was a dutiful, model child. The younger son enjoyed partying and hanging out with his

Table 17

friends. Rather than work, the younger son asked his father to divide the inheritance now and give him his share immediately. The father agreed. Now rich, the son went off to the big city and indulged in "sex, drugs, and rock 'n' roll." One day the money was gone, along with the "friends." To avoid starvation, the young man was forced into the lowliest of work, feeding hogs.

It dawned on him that the servants at his father's house ate better and lived better than he did now. He made up his mind to go home and throw himself on his father's mercy. He would ask for forgiveness and to be allowed to become a servant of his father.

As the young son approached the long driveway up to the house, the father spotted him and recognized him. He shouted with joy and called to the servants to begin preparing the most lavish meal possible with all the boy's favorite dishes. Then the father ran out with the best clothes in the house to put over the boy's rags.

In utter joy, the father disregarded the request to become like a servant, "You are my son who was lost to me. Now you are back. We celebrate!"

Through stories and actions, Jesus showed his followers what God is like: a God of love. Grounded in God's love for humanity, Jesus urged his followers to love God back. The most important thing in life, he said, quoting Hebrew scripture, is to respond to God's love with all your heart, soul, mind, and strength.[19] This principle was so important to him, he called it a commandment, one of only two he would give: to love God and to love each other.[20]

People who heard Jesus began to envision God as a caring parent to humanity, whose welcome is warm and generous to any who will come. Jesus told of this loving God in stories, and he acted out this same love in his own life. Jesus made it clear that he sat at table with anyone and everyone because he served a God who welcomes all.

The Welcoming Table

At the Scottsbluff picnic and fire circle, I did not knowingly rehearse all this in my mind. Rather, I remembered in an instant a lifetime of church meals and settings where I had heard the stories of

Jesus. In those settings, I had felt the hospitality of the table. I had been reminded that I was important—I was welcome—whether as a child or an adult.

Scottsbluff reminded me also of yet another table—one where the spirit is fed—a table called the communion table. It renews my spirit just like food renews my body.

In my denomination,[21] gathering at the communion table is a weekly tradition at the center of the Sunday worship. In simple gestures and words, it tells the story of Jesus. It tells how Jesus lived as a witness to God's love, how his absolute insistence on loving God and neighbor brought him into conflict with the civil and religious authorities. How, even though he could have recanted or just gone silent about the good news of God's embracing love for all, he simply kept on reaching out in God's name with that same love.

At the communion table, Christians particularly remember Jesus' Last Supper with his closest friends the night before he would be arrested and taken to trial. One of the descriptions of that night, the one told by John,[22] says that at that very supper Jesus was still finding ways to show the extravagance of God's love and welcome. As they gathered, Jesus literally took on the role of a servant. He wrapped a towel around his waist, picked up the water basin used to wash feet, and approached his disciples to wash the dusty grime off of theirs. He told them that if he, their teacher, could wash their feet, they should remember to serve anyone else themselves. Later that evening he made it even clearer: "I give you a new commandment, that you love one another. Just as I have loved you, you also should love one another. By this everyone will know that you are my disciples, if you have love for one another" (Jn. 13:34–35).

At the communion table, Christ's table, the Spirit of God gathers the community in the presence of this God of love, of radical welcome. At the table, whether we are more like the older, dutiful son or the younger prodigal, we are assured of God's embrace. We are reminded that, just as Jesus introduced to us a God of love, now we have the joy of living in that love, of sharing it with people around us, and introducing them to God as well.

Jesus' ministry was in great part intended to show in word and deed what God is like. God is a loving God who, like the householder, watches out for the most vulnerable family member; who, like the

Table 19

"father of the nation," leads the people out of slavery; who sets up a way of living where there is room for all and welcomes all of us into it. All of us! And the symbol of that welcome is the table.

A friend tells his daughter's story of working in Appalachia. There she met a family whose dinner table was set in their large kitchen. At that table they gathered for meals and sharing the news of the day. It was a rough-hewn, handmade table, the handiwork of the dad. Each time a new child was born into the family, he went out and cut another board for that table. They always made room for one more in their expanding family.[23]

The communion table also makes room for anyone who responds to the invitation of God's love. It stands as an infinitely expandable table through time and around the world.

I grew up knowing this in principle. One day it became real for me. I knew the new leaf had been added to the table with my name on it.

As God Has Welcomed Us

I was ready. So, that Palm Sunday I did it, with quaking knees and steady heart. I was eleven years old and nervous, but ready to "go forward"—to walk down that center aisle at church and stand before the whole congregation and have the pastor ask me, "Do you believe that Jesus is the Christ, the son of the living God and your Lord and Savior?"

I remember well the moment after. The hymn was sung. The question asked and answered. My pastor was holding my right hand in his two hands, leaning forward so he could look straight into my eyes. He said, "Jesus told us that whenever anyone here on earth confesses him before people, he will confess that person before God in heaven... Sharon, I think we know what Jesus is doing right now!"

Wow!

My heart soared! *Jesus knows* me. *Knows my name.* Growing up in the church, I already knew Jesus loves me. I'd sung that song[24] for as long as I could remember. And of course I loved Jesus back. That was the whole point of my walk up the aisle that morning. Even so, something about that moment and my pastor's confident assurance was different and immediate; it was real. Jesus was, right then, talking to God about me. I felt part of the family of God in a whole new, powerful way. Though I had been in church nearly every Sunday since my birth, that day I felt truly that this was my home. Not just this congregation, but wherever Christ's people were gathered.

Eventually, I would come to want this for all God's children—for everybody to feel that sense of secure belonging, where everyone's name is known, where all are valued just as they are: young or old, experienced or inexperienced, skilled or not, yet loved and cherished by name.

The love of God is never just for me, but for all. God's love is meant to be experienced and then to be shared. Followers of Christ have the opportunity to welcome others as God has welcomed us.

In today's global culture, the world seems smaller, but, ironically, people are often more separated and isolated from each other than ever. "Spiritual but not religious" results in part from living in a technological age in which we know more about all kinds of subjects even as we are less rooted in community. We have a flood of data available to us at all times, but not always the context to process it meaningfully. Access to information brings a new kind of vulnerability. Even the largest corporations and nations know that a single techno-hacker can stop large computer systems, leaving us all vulnerable to the lonely, disenfranchised individual. In such a world, the table speaks to our longing to be together, to find trust, to build community.

The frequent television caricatures of Christianity are about dividing lines and stating who's in and who's out. The spiritual heart of my denomination, however, is a table where all are welcome because a loving God first welcomed us. It is a family table and much more. Food of symbolic nature is shared, but more important is the timeless, boundless embrace of the table's host, who is Jesus.

Christianity at its best is more a network of relationships than a set of beliefs. It is about the relationship of individual Christians and Christian communities with a living God who they have come to know through Jesus. It is about the Spirit of God, which pervades all of life with divine love.

The table symbolizes the healing and wholeness of that love.

⸗⸗⸗ ⸗⸗⸗ ⸗⸗⸗

Table 21

Surprisingly, Hollywood has gotten this one right. In a movie entitled *Places in the Heart*,[25] a woman's husband is murdered. An unlikely array of individuals come together to bring in the cotton crop and save the widow's farm.

Toward the end of the movie, in a communion service, the bread and cup are passed from the blind man to the African American man to the white widow lady to…(and now comes the surprise) to her murdered husband who is somehow sitting on the row beside her. Now we know something unusual is happening here.

Then the woman's deceased husband passes the communion tray into the hands of the young man who was his murderer, and this is more than mere movie magic. The communion table has become a table open to all, a place for older brothers and younger brothers to meet, where enemies are reconciled. The table has bridged the gap of the violence that is between them. It calls out for reconciling love as they share the meal in the spirit of Christ still very much alive and present.

Most who gather at the table each week do not come as murderers. Many come as weary travelers through life. Some come looking for an answer to loneliness. Others come looking for forgiveness and renewal from deep brokenness. Still others simply need a respite from the daily strains of life. The longing may be as yet unarticulated, as in the case of the woman at my office door. Yet we gather.

There is something about being invited to the table, especially the communion table. That table is the center of spiritual renewal, of personal affirmation. It is the most welcoming place of all. At that table is the welcome of God.

QUESTIONS

Chapter 1

1. Recall tables that have been important in your life. Why were they important? Was it the food, family activities, experiencing friendship, special celebrations, or other unusual events or activities?

2. How did Jesus use meals (sometimes with tables and sometimes without tables) in his ministry with people?

3. What meanings do the communion table and communion service convey? To long-time members? To newcomers? To you?

4. Have you met people who long to find God but are uncomfortable with churches? What would you want to say to them about God?

5. In what ways does your church show that God is love?

2

Welcome

We Welcome All to the Lord's Table

Basking in God's Love

Gentle waves lapping on the Irish shore had become the rolling swells of the Atlantic Ocean. Our twelve-person fishing boat dipped and rose with them. Not enough to make us nervous, not quite. Even on this sunny day, and still in sight of land, we were aware that in a less favorable season, this short journey could be dangerous. Good fortune smiled on our family that day; the waves and currents permitted the trip.

Skellig Michael's jagged contour grew more apparent as we approached. We could make out patches of green scattered across the crags. Some of the stone steps came into view, a rugged stairway that we would climb to get to the top of the 218-meter high island.[1] In the sixth century, Irish monks had retreated to this isolated rock to worship only God. We intended to retrace their steps.

The monks had set out for Skellig Michael to venerate God. They had experienced the power of God's welcome and had stood in awe before the grace of it. They reciprocated with passion. They longed to pour out their love directly to God from dawn to dusk, undistracted by anything else. They determined to give their whole lives, every waking minute, back to God.

Their companions were wind and water, sky and rain, and occasionally sun. Painstakingly over many years, the brothers hauled rocks to the top of the island and arranged them into human-sized "beehive" habitations. A capstone or wooden slab at the top of each circular dwelling kept it from toppling in. The guidebook descriptions did not make them sound very stable, but the evidence spoke for itself. The beehives were still standing. By contrast, the nearby twelfth-century church had been built on a more familiar pattern, with a wooden roof topping vertical walls at right angles to each other. The church knelt in ruins, roofless.

The beehives gave mute testimony that even these hermit monks needed a connection with community. In the silence of their devotion, it still took common work to grow and prepare food, to build shelter, to be the visible place where the spirit could dwell. They built a monastery of rock beehives so that they could live together.

In their intention to love God purely and completely, the monks drew strength in community.

———⟨⟨⟨⟩⟩⟩———   ———⟨⟨⟨⟩⟩⟩———   ———⟨⟨⟨⟩⟩⟩———

Jesus' life was shaped by a rhythm of both personal devotion to God and life in community with his twelve disciples. Biblical stories tell that he often withdrew for quiet times of prayer to be recharged for his life in community and his forays back among the crowds.

———⟨⟨⟨⟩⟩⟩———   ———⟨⟨⟨⟩⟩⟩———   ———⟨⟨⟨⟩⟩⟩———

My first awareness of the interplay between spirit and community took place at church camp. For a week each summer in junior and senior high, young Disciples from all over the state retreated from daily life to live in Christian community for six days. Hiking, swimming, intense discussion, singing (including some of the same songs my bicycle companions and I would later sing at a Nebraska campfire) filled the week. My circle of friends looked forward to it all year long.

Morning Watch began each day: a time set aside to find a quiet place to pray individually and reconnect personally with God. The natural world provided the backdrop: brilliant greens of the meadow in the play of shadow and sun, golden hay bales scattered across the fields, the early morning buzz of insects, my own breathing as I took in the beauty of God's creation. Gratitude swept over me. In a tiny way, like the monks at Skellig Michael, my own sense of welcome at God's table was renewed by daily mini-withdrawals at camp.

The solitude came to an end with the breakfast bell. In a moment or two our ears would be filled with shouts and laughter and the scraping of metal chairs on linoleum tile as we found our seats in front of pancakes or eggs. For the rest of the day the voice of God would speak, not through silence, but through interaction with our campmates and counselors as we reflected on God's love for us and our returning of that love.

***

God communicates love through living, breathing people in community, whether through Abraham's family, the tribes of Israel, the voices of biblical prophets, sixth-century Irish monks, or high school young people at church camp. Zacchaeus got the message sitting at dinner with Jesus. My church community first introduced me to God's love by loving me and by welcoming me to Christ's communion table.

The experience of Christian community at camp helped me go deeper than the warm glow of merely feeling welcomed myself. As we campers reflected on our own life together for that week, we began to believe God means for something this wonderful to be shared with others. We left camp determined to extend God's welcome, to find opportunities to add a leaf or two of our own to this welcome table.

Loving God by Welcoming Neighbor

The university campus that houses the seminary I attended is dotted with buildings intended to communicate mystery. Known as "secret societies," they are windowless; a person standing outside cannot see in. On wintry, overcast New England days, these buildings can send some imaginations wandering down a pretty creepy path. Other imaginations, tantalized by anything deemed "off limits," begin to devise a way in. Only the initiated are allowed inside these most exclusive of clubs.

The church operates on a different model—one of broad, expansive welcome. At least, it is supposed to. Sadly, sometimes the reality is that the most precious Christian traditions, including the hospitality of the communion table itself, mystify people not used to experiencing them. Without mediation, these traditional acts communicate the opposite of welcome and seem more like a secret society than a wide-open table.

One congregation I served as pastor wanted to throw wide the church doors to our neighbors. We wished for our friends to experience the same love and renewal we perceived each week around that table.

We suspected an unintended mystery factor about Christian practice stood as a dis-invitation to the uninitiated. So we devised a strategy. We started inviting people to a more familiar table: the dinner table.

Our plan[2] was based on two basic characteristics of our church community: first, we thoroughly enjoyed being together; and, second, we loved to eat! So, how better to introduce ourselves to our neighbors than by inviting them to dinner?

Of course, it meant that the people of the church had a great time, too. In March, an Irish band and line dancers got us all stepping to the music. In May we celebrated Cinco de Mayo with a Mexican band and our favorite Tex-Mex recipes. Dancing was involved that time, too…as well as a piñata for the kids.

Our welcome to our friends and neighbors was genuine. We also believed that once our guests participated in the fun of a Friday night, they would be curious to see where we hung out on Sunday. Having invited them to the dinner table, we would be ready to welcome them to that other table, too—the communion table. Through our hospitality, our neighbors would be opened to the welcoming embrace of God.

We were following in a long tradition of people who have met Jesus.

—◦/◦/◦—   —◦/◦/◦—   —◦/◦/◦—

Once in the middle of a typically hot, dusty day on foot, Jesus sent his disciples on ahead into town to find some lunch.[3] He himself approached a well seeking a moment of quiet and a cool drink. He came across a woman filling a jug of water, which was unusual at this time of day. They fell into conversation, which was also unusual. Men and women in that culture normally did not address each other in public.

By the time the disciples returned, the woman had become convinced this was no ordinary traveler, but a man of God. His understanding of her situation had changed her life, she said. The disciples would hear none of it. Couldn't they leave Jesus to his own devices for one minute? Here he was, once again, disregarding basic social do's and don'ts, associating with this random woman. As they scolded, the woman departed, unnoticed. She ran into town. She told everyone she met about this person who had given her life a new beginning, who made her feel respected and worthy of love.

Through her encounter with Jesus, the woman at the well had caught the Spirit of God's love. No one could have blamed her if she had wanted to just sit back and bask in it. She did not sit back. Much like people who want to display new Christmas presents to friends and acquaintances after the holiday, the woman at the well wanted her neighbors to see what she had received. She wasted no time running to tell them of her experience!

My congregation shared our gratitude for God's love and demonstrated our love for God by inviting others to the table: first to our dinner table and then to God's table. We invited them into our community of worship and devotion. As beautiful as the spiritual table of God is, however, offering an invitation to come into the spiritual life within a particular community is just a beginning. Christian community is not merely a retreat to concentrate on experiencing God's love. God's love experienced in Christian community changes us. It turns our attention outward and becomes the ground on which we learn to share God's love outside of the church community.

Reaching Out—Building Community

At last! I pulled a chair up to the dinner table after a long, hard shift at the Women's Blitz Build in Beaumont, Texas. The folks at Habitat for Humanity[4] had assured us we could build a house in a single week. We had given it our best start on that initial day.

The morning had starkly reminded me of the last build I had been on. That time, back in Oklahoma, I had discovered that I basically couldn't hammer a nail. "Tap, tap, tap, tap, tap, tap, tap," my hammer would plead with the nail. Meanwhile, the more confident retired gentleman next to me would already have a couple driven into place, each with a loud, "Pound! Pound!" So this day I had made my contribution by holding pink painted lumber in place for others to hammer. Was it a particular "Women's Build" shade of pink or just a coincidental color? I did not know. Anyway, with fifty-one Disciples women working alongside the future owner of the home, stacks of it had morphed into the frame of a house by late afternoon. Now, at the dinner hour, my muscles were tired though not yet screaming; that was for tomorrow.

Habitat for Humanity projects had punctuated my church life. I remembered fresh-faced, enthusiastic college students on Spring Break who had descended on Bartlesville, Oklahoma, to help build houses there. Our congregation hosted them annually for meals with Sloppy Joes, chips, lemonade, cookies. The young idealists, however briefly, brought a contagious energy and good humor.

Our own congregation's youth once built a life-sized playhouse for the backyard of a new Habitat home across town. Our children took pleasure in constructing a safe place for youngsters of another community to play.

I thought about that moment when a Habitat family receives the keys to their new house in the presence of the volunteers who have helped build it. All share a sense of pride. New owners enjoy a sense of being part of a new community. The volunteers know that their own community has been strengthened doing something together for and with others. Owners and volunteers alike feel more fully at home.

Now I was at table in yet another church. We women of the Blitz Build were the guests here, receiving the hospitality of Northwood Christian Church as we worked to rebuild a neighborhood in Beaumont. It felt like tables and communities within other communities; like a Russian nesting doll being opened to reveal another doll that opens to reveal yet another doll. In the center of this experience rested God's welcoming love: food for the spirit served up in community.

—◊◊◊— —◊◊◊— —◊◊◊—

I believe it is a natural response to return love to a loving God. Basking in that love, pulling up a chair at God's table, so to speak, follows Jesus's model of loving God with heart, soul, mind, and strength.

Jesus also asks more. He instructs his followers to stand up from the table, as well. His own life showed that we love God by reaching out and actively loving our neighbors where they are, not just by inviting them into our space. Proclaiming in words, "God loves you and so do I," is not a sufficient demonstration of love. Words of love require evidence to be believable. God's love requires self-giving by both individuals and communities as modeled by Jesus. Love in action is why my congregation became so involved with Habitat for Humanity. It is why all these Disciples women from all across the country had descended upon Beaumont for the Blitz Build.

Offering ourselves to others out of love for them has an unintended side effect as well. Even as we share community with others, our own lives are enriched. Our community is deepened. Learning to love our neighbor is part of the transformation in our own lives, which happens when we rest in God's powerful love. We feel ourselves becoming more like Jesus, who reached out to people from all walks of life, who sat at table with them.

The "all walks of life" part sometimes gets challenging, however. Jesus said the one who shows mercy is a neighbor. The truth is we cannot always choose our neighbors.

Love in Action

Days of warning had not prepared anyone for this: winds howling to category 5, levies breached, mile after mile of roofs blown away, streets flooded.

As Hurricane Katrina bore down on Moss Point, Mississippi, Ann Pickett took shelter and waited out the storm.

When the clouds cleared, she emerged to see the damage. Up and down the street her neighbors also appeared, standing stunned. Jaws dropped.

Ann thought about her wedding, only days away. What did she do? She went to church, but not just to bow her head and pray.

She took the wedding food from her own freezer and, in the church kitchen, she started to cook for her neighbors! Ann and her fiancé cooked up their wedding feast for any who came.

Ann prepared that meal on her own initiative, but she offered it in the spirit of a loving God. She served her meal from a location that bore the name of Jesus Christ: Moss Point Christian Church.

Truth be told, disasters often bring out the best in human beings. After flood and tornado and hurricane, news outlets recount tale after tale of people putting aside differences and reaching out to help their neighbors.

Ann launched into action because she calls herself Christian. She set a table out of Christian love for her neighbors, any and all, following the example of Jesus.

———————— ———————— ————————

The posters on the walls of Mexican buildings in border towns say starkly in Spanish: "Don't even try it!" The graphic portrays a map of the southern United States splashed with blood-red dots. Each one stands for a person who has paid the ultimate price trying to cross the Sonoran Desert on foot. Half-circles mark the distances from the starting point: one day in, two days in, three days in. Clusters of dots paint splotches in all sections. The cause of death is varied. Gunshot wounds take a smaller number, but most die of exposure in the winter or of dreadful thirst in the brutally hot summer.

Some, with strength to carry them and good fortune to keep them out of the crosshairs and away from animals and snakes, make it to the most elemental "table" of all: a drum of life-sustaining, life-saving water.

The network of 65 gallon water drums is maintained by hundreds of volunteers, many of them church-goers, including those from First Christian Church, Tucson. They work together through an organization called Humane Borders.[5] Their purpose is to set a table of life, in their case for perfect strangers, in the name of a loving God.

———————— ———————— ————————

The jogger stopped at the church to chat with the pastor.[6] He reported, "I've heard that you all are a great church. I believe that you have the ideal location for a soup kitchen." (Close to a bus stop; not far from downtown; easy to find.) He continued, "If you start a soup kitchen here, I would help you get started, and I would cook for it."

It didn't take long for this Christian church to accept the offer of the Jewish jogger. Together they set up the soup kitchen and began reaching out to the homeless community in their town.

———∽ⅉⅉⅉⅉ∽—— ——∽ⅉⅉⅉ∽—— ——∽ⅉⅉⅉ∽——

Why would these people set these tables for strangers?

Ann Pickett and activists through Humane Borders and First Christian Church, Charlotte, North Carolina, had themselves been welcomed to tables of God's love. They knew there is a link between love and action, between community and spirit, between body and soul. They could see that love received from God pours out into loving action, sometimes as basic as offering a meal to otherwise unknown, seemingly random, people. They learned it from Jesus.

———∽ⅉⅉⅉ∽—— ——∽ⅉⅉⅉ∽—— ——∽ⅉⅉⅉ∽——

Jesus was teaching his twelve disciples, along with a crowd of over 5000 people.[7] His reputation was spreading, and the crowds were getting larger. As the day progressed, the disciples worried about how to feed such a crowd. They pulled Jesus aside and suggested he dismiss the people and let them go into town to find food. To the disciples' consternation, their leader replied, "You give them something to eat." Even as they were shaking their heads in dismay, a little boy stepped forward with arms outstretched, offering them his own lunch. It wouldn't feed many: only five loaves of bread and two fish. Still, he gave it to share with the crowd. Jesus received the food, prayed over it, and started passing bread and fish around.

The bread and fish did not run out. All ate, with plenty left over. It all started with the generosity and trust of one young person.

Some who know this story believe that the boy's act in the presence of Jesus motivated people throughout the crowd to reveal their own packed lunches. Those shared lunches added up to a feast for all, with food to spare. Others insist that a supernatural event of multiplication happened that day; Jesus' touch and prayer literally expanded that small lunch into enough for a crowd.

Either way, Jesus' instructions to the disciples allowed no compromise. "You give them something to eat." When the little boy stepped forward and did just that, it turned out there was more than enough. No excuses. Jesus knew what he was talking about. The people needed to eat, and the capacity to meet the situation already existed among them.

Moments after Katrina roared through Moss Point, Ann Pickett acted in the spirit of Jesus' words. "You give them something to eat." And she did. She offered food to all her neighbors. Love in action—a physical sign of a spiritual value.

The church people of Tucson were paying attention to Jesus' example. He ate even with strangers. These Arizona Christians started with the basics. They set out plain water for people they would never meet, on a most elemental table: the desert floor.

The people of Charlotte, North Carolina, worked with someone outside their own faith community to serve meals for homeless people in their community. They had heard the words of Jesus about God's love for everyone. They knew they had to respond in kind.

All had experienced the welcome of God at multiple tables, including the communion table. Something was now required of them. They reached out to provide hospitality for others as well. They served real food to flesh and blood people who otherwise might have gone without. Spirit and body are connected. Hungry people can't hear a message of love. Passing the word along effectively begins with tangible acts of care.

A respected Christian leader in Democratic Republic of Congo used to give advice especially to missionaries who were there to "share Jesus' message of God's love." He would say, "It's not enough to reach the soul of a person; you have to reach the whole of a person."[8]

Words of love do not ring true without acts of love.

Christian community is partly spiritual, centered on the presence of a loving God introduced to us by Jesus. Christian community is also human. It is love in action in the model of Jesus. It expands the circle, seeking out new ways to share that love with more people.

Truth in advertising, however: at that point of expansion, the original community will be changed. When enough new leaves are added to the table, eventually the whole kitchen has to expand.

Expanding the Neighborhood

My husband and I raised our two kids in a great neighborhood in Enid, Oklahoma.

In the spring, the parents hid Easter eggs in the park for a grand, neighborhood-wide Easter egg hunt. In the winter, several of the families went Christmas caroling in the neighborhood. (Every year, at Martha and Harold Hatt's house, we sang, "Hark, the Harold Hatt we sing…" We laughed at our own weak pun every time.)

I grew up in a similar neighborhood in Indianapolis a generation earlier. Everybody looked after everybody else. One day our next-door neighbor's son was playing at our house, and he fell off the porch, gashing his head open. As with any head wound, blood flowed. His parents weren't at home, so we gathered him up and rushed him to the emergency room. Of course we did! Anybody would have done that.

In Indianapolis and Enid both, we "neighbors" took care of each other in need. We also borrowed cups of sugar, visited across the back fence, and sat on each other's front porches on long summer evenings. We were neighbors in a casual sort of way.

But that is not how Jesus uses the term "neighbor."[9] In Jesus' eyes, it is the guy from the other side of the tracks, the good Samaritan, who shows us how to be neighborly. He became the neighbor when he bundled up the stranger who was in need and took him to get the necessary care. In Jesus' story, the one who shows mercy is the neighbor, next-door or not.

Jesus seriously expands the concept of "neighborhood" here. In Jesus' dictionary, a "neighbor" does not necessarily live close by. For Jesus, the neighbor is the one who shows mercy to others, wherever they may live.

Churches can resemble either kind of neighborhood. They can get very cozy in their own community, as I was in Enid and Indianapolis. Everyone knows everyone else. Activities focus on loving God and loving each other, who we all know so well. In fact, some schools of thought say that churches should consist of "like" people: same class, same culture, same ages. Churches grow in contexts of "sameness," the theory goes.[10]

Jesus seems to have had something different in mind. In expanding the neighborhood, people of differing class, differing culture, differing ages come into contact with each other. On his very first "inaugural" day, after reading from the scroll, Jesus said to his listeners, essentially, "This message does not belong just to us. It is for everyone, maybe for others even more than for us."[11] He was expanding the neighborhood. Remember: whoever shows mercy…

A similar message comes through in the feeding of the 5000. When all those people ate bread and fish, the miracle was not only in how many people were fed. The miracle was also which people were fed. All the people were fed, including the poor, rich, sick and quarantined, revolutionaries, and soldiers: all. These people normally would not have gotten along with each other. But their differences or their relative social status did not concern Jesus. He showed that all the people were welcome at that wide-open field of a table. All needed to eat, and all received their needed food.

God's welcome of us leads us to reach out and extend hospitality to other people, even people who might otherwise be separate from each other. As children of God in God's embrace, we discover in ourselves a basic humanity that unites us all.

It is not necessarily easy to love God by loving our neighbor. Our "neighbor," as Jesus defines the term in the good Samaritan story, might be a stranger to us, might not be "like" us, might be someone who would ordinarily spark suspicion or even fear in us. Loving our neighbor can require more from us than we originally intended. That is where the transformation comes in.

Transformation

The buzz of conversation met the visitors before they completely descended the steps into the church basement. The smell of cooking food overcame the end-of-day odors emanating from the gathered throng.

It was a motley crew.

A bearded seminary professor, various retired faculty persons from the nearby university, and church member volunteers from different walks of life chatted with people from the town. Originally the townsfolk came as guests to this weekly dinner. Several years into it, however, the Mamre meal[12] had developed its own community. Folks arrived by bus, on foot, and a few carpooled. Word of mouth spread the invitation.

A closer look revealed the worn shoes, mismatched clothes, broken teeth, and stooped postures of poverty. Just beyond the laughter and chatter of the moment, furrowed brows and worried expressions made ready to take their habitual place on faces. Denied disability checks, exhausted food stamps, the long trip across state to the VA hospital, the drag of mental illness all dogged these people in various combinations.

At the Mamre meal, "guests" could also show a more empowered side of themselves. Some participated in the cooking and serving. It was hard to tell by role who was guest and who was host. The meal belonged to everyone now. The integrated nature of the community became even more obvious, and more touching, as the community sat down to eat. At these tables, not only food was shared, but also personal knowledge and experience.

The meal had some ritual to it. Loosely based on a communion service, they thanked God and broke bread together. They remembered that Jesus broke bread with his friends, especially at the most difficult moment of his life. They recalled that Jesus had asked his followers to do the same.

Later, as the Mamre meal progressed, community members lifted a cup of water, iced tea, or lemonade, and thanked God for life. They also prayed for each other and for the challenges of their lives. And then came the most life-giving moment of all. In the midst of a meal offered for "the poor," the very same persons heard the concerns and worries of their friends, and spoke up to offer each other advice and help. "I know a free clinic where there's a doctor who will see you." "My friend has a couch he'll let you sleep on." "My brother can give you a ride." "I have a coat you can have."

The original congregation took pride in the Tuesday night Mamre meal. In reaching out to offer hospitality to the poor, the church was doing just what it ought to do. The Mamre folk felt the welcome. So much so, that one or two decided to check out the Sunday service.

That's when things got complicated.

No one exactly objected when the first gentleman started attending and eventually came forward to formally become part of the congregation. His membership did give one or two of the long-time church members furrowed brows of their own. Most, however, saw his presence as affirmation that the Mamre meal was genuinely communicating God's love.

When several more of the Mamre folk came upstairs and then several more, the challenge became apparent. The character of the

Sunday morning service began to change. Alongside the stillness and folded hands of middle class "propriety," the newcomers spontaneously popped up and down to handle spur-of-the-moment impulses. The quiet, introspective, formal worship was now interrupted by a counterpoint of full voice commentary and exclamation.

It began to dawn on the eleven o'clock crowd that to extend the neighborhood meant the neighborhood would change.

———⚬/\/\/⚬——— ———⚬/\/\/⚬——— ———⚬/\/\/⚬———

Jesus' message about the expanding neighborhood was challenging even in his time. On the day of his "inaugural speech," in his own hometown, he almost immediately got into trouble.

At first it was going well. "Isn't this Jesus? Joseph and Mary's son? Look how he's grown, how well-spoken he is."

"Listen to the beautiful passage he's chosen to read from the Bible. I like that message: promising us release from the things that bind us."

"Yeah, down with Roman occupation!"

"My hip could use some healing, that's for sure!"

And then Jesus had to go and spoil a good thing. "Oh, you thought this message was for you?" he asked. "God has a record of reaching beyond us to people we don't even like." He went on to mention specific instances when God had reached out to the people of Lebanon and Syria.[13] "God will do so again. This message goes way beyond just us."

His commentary did not sit very well with the home folks. Now Jesus had gone too far. They ran him out of town that very day.

Jesus did not change his message, however.

God's love is for all God's children. Those who get the message first, who have the privilege of experiencing God's love early, now have the opportunity to love God back by loving God's other children. These early adopters discover their true humanity as children of God as they reach out in self-giving love even to strangers, as they expand the "neighborhood," extending the community of care. True, such expressions of God's love change the original community, often challenging the community with unwanted transformation.

Such transformation can also be life itself.

True Community

The predominantly Anglo congregation in Coral Gables, Florida, was following an all-too-familiar path. More of their neighbors these days spoke Spanish than English. Many church members now drove in from quite a distance for worship. An increasing number were old enough that the drive itself was becoming a challenge.

Then Central Christian Church took the bold step of calling a pastor whose childhood home was Puerto Rico. Now at least someone could talk to the neighbors!

The Rev. Jorge Cotto proved fluent not only in both English and Spanish. His gift of communication included helping people bridge culture and generation gaps. The congregation had already shown their willingness to extend the community by inviting the leadership of their new pastor. With his insight and skill, they also figured out how to adjust their familiar practices in order to make worship and fellowship more hospitable to the surrounding community. Church attendance began to climb.

Eventually, the newer members predominated. By that time, though, the culture of the congregation had evolved to a point of celebrating diversity itself as a gift. It showed. Some new members were African American and Anglo from the U.S. Others were from the Caribbean, South and Central America, and Europe: a truly multi-cultural, international mix. Newer members continued to love and respect and welcome the gifts of the long-time members. In the words of their pastor, "'CCC Gables is one local congregation represented by many nationalities, cultures, languages, and generations, but with one pastor, one board, one budget, and one vision. 'We are One.'"[14]

Loving God by loving others can require sacrifice. Expanding the neighborhood can also become its own reward.

———

First Christian Church, Oaktown, is located in one of the poorest counties in Indiana.[15] Their sixty-five members, mostly retired, join every summer with the United Methodist Church to host Vacation

Church School—for the neighborhood children. In the fall, the two churches make sure those kids have backpacks full of school supplies. First Christian Church also hosts a Wednesday night supper for the children throughout the school year, including games and children-oriented worship, again mostly for children who are not members of the church.

That is only the beginning of their outreach. Oaktown sits in the middle of melon country. Migrant workers harvest their "best melons in the state." First Christian Church noticed. "The workers need Spanish language Bibles," they thought, "to be sure they know about the love of God and the stories of Jesus." The church soon realized that love in action required more evidence. They organized other churches to join with them in reaching out to the workers with free medical and dental clinics and English language lessons.

Then the folks at Oaktown saw that permanent residents of the community, too, had some of the same needs. So they organized with their partners a year-round local outreach, much like they had already begun with the migrant workers.

This quiet congregation of retired people now reverberates with the sounds of children, especially on Wednesday nights. They reach out to neighbors across the county, partnering with whoever will. When trucks pull up to their church building during the week to unload pallets of canned goods for the food pantry, inmates from the county jail do the unloading. Church members connect with neighbors in town and in the surrounding towns and cities, building coalitions that give evidence to the God of love who first loved them.

It takes a lot of energy. Their own lives are sometimes turned upside down. But they are humming with life, filled with joy, amazed at how God's circle can expand and transform them.

<hr />

In San Diego, Casa de Oración (CDO) lives their prayers.[16] Three worship services in two languages and a new church start in Fullerton testify to the outreach of this House of Prayer. Love in action from this congregation crosses national boundaries. It starts with the palpable welcome to all who cross the threshold. Meals are shared; a sense of community extends in friendship and faith.

Some who arrive at Casa de Oración have learned by hard experience to test an apparent welcome in this border city. They are not citizens, but, for too many reasons to name, they are in the United States without visa or Green Card. At CDO, Pastor Xosé Escamilla sees to it they find a church home.

But sometimes not for long.

For too many, the specter of deportation becomes real. They find themselves dropped with nothing but the clothes on their back on the Tijuana side of the border, separated from family and friends.

That's where Pastor Guadalupe "Lupita" Castillo and her congregation, Iglesia de Todas las Naciones, in Tijuana come in. Pastor Lupita sets a welcoming table in Mexico, at her own home, now a church and welcome center, as well. Church members pick up these disoriented people, bring them to shelter, feed them, and begin the process of helping them get back on their feet.

The twin congregations reach back and forth, supporting families, giving spiritual support and social encouragement to people caught in the thicket of unreformed U.S. immigration law. The entwined lives of these Mexican and U.S. communities cross human-made national borders with the love of God. It expands their own sense of who they are, defined less by nationality than by the community of Jesus' expanded neighborhood.

Diana Butler Bass describes the woman who looks with joy at her incredibly diverse congregation, people who wouldn't ordinarily gather together, and says, "So, here's an opportunity to have real community."[17]

Because, where is the witness to the power of God's love if you only love people you would be with anyway?

Discovering Ourselves

The Habitat for Humanity story began in Americus, Georgia. There Clarence Jordan had developed a Christian, racially integrated community (much to the consternation of the local population). Clarence, along with new residents Millard and Linda Fuller, came up with an idea. They figured that with a combination of volunteer labor, sweat equity from owners, and interest-free loans, many more people could have decent, affordable housing. Almost immediately they started building houses at Americus.

It might have ended there, but for the Fullers and a partnership with the Christian Church (Disciples of Christ). Their joint venture expanded the neighborhood beyond Americus—way beyond, as it turned out. The Disciples appointed the Fullers as missionaries to a little brick-making project in Mbandaka, Zaire,[18] bricks that could be used to build houses. Zaire was a land of complicated relationships between rich and poor, a land of extraordinary natural wealth and even more extraordinary corruption and despair. However, Mbandaka was the seat of a strong and thriving Disciples church. From within that community of Zairian Disciples, using bricks from the brick-making project, the first Habitat for Humanity community was begun.

———

The Mbandaka Habitat for Humanity account is the story of a community transformed. It is also a symbol of hope for a world renewed.

The plot of land given for the initial Habitat project in Zaire was available because of its checkered past. Named Bokotola, it had long existed as the no-man's land, the "sanitation zone" between white and black Mbandaka of colonial times. The name itself meant "the person who does not like others."[19]

As Zairians and international volunteers working together built house after house, however, it became clear a new community was developing. Bokotola needed a new name. In beautiful contrast to the old meaning, the new name selected was Losanganya: "reconciler, reunifier, everyone together."

———

In the deep spirituality of the table, Jesus reveals to us a God of love. In the true community of an expanding neighborhood, God introduces us to the loving humanity we can be. We learn to recognize our best selves, part of an extended neighborhood of love in action.

Those expanded communities, however, are not the end of the story until they are as big as the world made new and whole.

QUESTIONS

Chapter 2

1. Remember times when you withdrew into solitude or silence to deal with stress or to regain your sense of direction. What did you do? Pray, read, calm all thoughts, turn off everything, read from the Bible, listen to music, spend time outdoors? What helps you "go deeper" during your times of individual communion with God?

2. In your experience, how does personal communion with God relate to experiences of God in community or to more public sharing of God's love?

3. What are some distinctive marks of hospitality as Christians practice it?

4. What are some ways that you and your church could "expand the neighborhood"? What would be the challenges? What would be the blessings?

3

Wholeness
Wholeness in a Fragmented World

Thankfully, World War II had ended. Hitler was defeated. Yet, in the midst of celebration, Christians lamented. They had engaged in a tragic war against each other, a devastating failure in witnessing to a God of love. Their thoughts began to focus on a specific prayer Jesus[1] had uttered just before his death. He had prayed fervently that after he was gone his followers would join together. He poured out to God his heartfelt desire that the world would see his disciples living as one, and, as a result, all would trust in the vision he had lived and strive to emulate it.

War-weary twentieth-century followers of Jesus made up their minds to become an answer to Jesus' prayer. They banded together across nationality and denomination into councils of churches as a step toward fulfilling a loving God's desire for oneness worldwide. They founded the World Council of Churches (WCC) and national councils as signs of their intent to live in reconciliation and unity. The Greek word *oikouménē*, meaning "the whole inhabited universe," gave the movement a name: "the ecumenical movement."

Not everyone caught the vision. From the beginning and until now opposing voices have expressed mistrust of the movement's purposes.

————— ————— —————

November 2013: Busan, Korea. He could see that the woman was going to throw something. As one hard-boiled egg whizzed past his ear, she reached into her pocket for another. He ducked in time to nearly miss getting hit square in the forehead. She had a pretty good aim!

The 10th Assembly of the World Council of Churches had finished. Just moments ago, those same eggs had been presented in great solemnity by members of the Korea Council of Churches to assembly-goers as a sign of hospitality and welcome. Now one of the demonstrators who had been on site for days had gotten hold of some of the eggs and was expressing her disagreement with the WCC's theology and aims, as much as she understood them. In her eyes the WCC represented syncretistic, communist leanings, and she wanted none of it in her country.

Ironically, her opposition to the WCC grew out of what many others think is one of its greatest moments. In perhaps their crowning achievement, twentieth-century ecumenists, seeking unity, helped bring an end to one of the post-war evils of that age

————— ————— —————

After years of apartheid[2] in South Africa, hope for a new era filled the news. Exhausted by the often violent struggle, buoyed by the recent release from prison of Nelson Mandela, the people approached an election. Ecumenical partners within South Africa and around the globe had been instrumental in bringing this day to pass.

The struggle for justice and freedom had become divisive even in the churches. In some cases, white Afrikaners were members of the same Christian denominations as black and "coloured" people. But being "brothers and sisters in Christ" did not stop the arrests or the beatings. Nor did it stop the sometimes equally violent response.

During those difficult years, international church networks, including the WCC, had reached out to South African Christians of color. In one particularly powerful moment, the South Africa Council of Churches was itself on trial for its anti-apartheid work.

Then something happened that changed that power equation. A sudden stir in the public gallery heralded a new group of visitors. Coming into the room were representatives of the World Council of Churches, the Archbishop of Canterbury, [and other Christian world leaders]… [T]he church of God from around the world had come to stand with its brothers and sisters in South Africa. Those of us involved in the struggle found new strength, certain that in the power of God, we would overcome.[3]

Conventional political and social lines blurred for people in the worldwide ecumenical movement; they saw the fundamental humanity of all South Africans. As elections drew near, coalitions of the churches together with some business leaders set the rules which helped to keep the elections peaceful. In one particularly telling moment, on the evening of the elections, the president of the South African Council of Churches took a phone call. Could he provide 800 church people *tomorrow* to count the vote? "These are the only people the parties will agree upon," the caller said. Through telephone chains, they were able to gather 1200.[4]

Years later, when the WCC 8th Assembly took place in Harare, Zimbabwe, Nelson Mandela delivered a major address. There he said:

[Y]ou have to have been in an apartheid prison in South Africa to appreciate the further importance of the church. They tried to isolate us completely from the outside. Our relatives could see us only once every six months. The link was religious organizations—Christians, Muslims, Hindus and members of the Jewish faith. They were the faithful who inspired us.

The WCC's support exemplified in the most concrete way the contribution that religion made to our liberation…[5]

The end had come to the cruel, splintering policy of apartheid. The country took a giant step in the direction toward wholeness.

Unfortunately, some never stopped believing that the connection with the liberation struggle amounted to support for communism. Thirty years later they were still showing their disapproval by throwing eggs.

In other parts of the twenty-first–century world, the problem for the ecumenical movement is not opposition but indifference.

———————

Around the table, persons spoke one after the other. "I never learned about the ecumenical movement in my congregation," one young person said. "I never taught it," said a pastor. "It doesn't interest anyone; all this church merger stuff. I'm sure it was important once upon a time, but I don't see it now."

Shock showed on the faces of the seniors in the room. What about Jesus' prayer? How could a group of leaders from the Disciples denomination, founded on the hope for Christian unity, say such things? How could they confuse particular strategies like institutional merger with the bedrock principle of oneness in Christ?

After further conversation, a tentative conclusion emerged. Perhaps the concept of Christian unity itself did not inspire the yawns. Perhaps it was the language used in talking about it.

———————

The drafting team re-entered the room. The smiles on their faces proclaimed their confidence that they had successfully completed their task. "We are disciples of Christ, a movement for *wholeness*," they proclaimed.

The others in the room listened and joined in their smiles: yes, "wholeness." Christian unity transcends mere institutional merger or accepting the lowest common denominator. It always has. The language of wholeness, indicating a unity that encompasses the healing of individuals and communities as well as churches, woke up the room.

———————

"Wholeness" meaning unity, and also completeness, healing, integrity, seemed to take.

A local pastor in southern California introduced the phrase, "a movement for wholeness in a fragmented world," to a group of middle school youngsters at his church. He asked them: "What does wholeness mean to you? Where do you see the world broken, and how can we have a mission of wholeness?"

They brainstormed for a while. Then the church gave each child $50.00 and told them to use it in a mission of bringing wholeness into their world. Several weeks later, by the end of that class, those young people had collectively turned their $50 each into $10,000 dollars' worth of good works!

They were named as their local community's philanthropists of the year! A middle school movement for wholeness in a fragmented world.

A look at the world can bring either fragmentation or wholeness into view…

Picture a globe—the kind of globe you have may have seen in a classroom: a model of earth set on an axis so that it can spin. Clear, stark lines delineate national borders. Contrasting colors for neighboring countries make sure each one stands distinct. This is Earth, as humans have drawn it.

Now, picture planet Earth as viewed in that iconic photograph taken from outside the earth's atmosphere. See the beautiful, multi-colored jewel—blue, green, brown, white—set on the rich black velvet backdrop of space. Many colors, yet one: Earth in the photo appears as God created it—without dividing lines, whole.

Church communities, formed in the image and the love of God, seek to reflect planet Earth rather than the line-riddled classroom globe. We strive to welcome all, blurring human-made boundaries, expanding the neighborhood at Jesus' instruction. We yearn for an experience of wholeness: unity, reconciliation, peace, and justice.

Wholeness begins as persons enfolded into God's welcome learn to love God back by loving neighbors near and far. And yet, the cozy communities that result from loving God and neighbor do not cue the final credits in the story. The happy ending has not quite arrived. God seems to have an even larger purpose in view: not just churches renewed, not just neighborhoods renewed; rather, a *world* renewed. Jesus said to go into all the world, making disciples.[6] Jesus' followers are called to introduce God's larger vision of wholeness for the entire world. Those who have caught the vision see that the story is just beginning to unfold. The next installment involves agreeing to participate in God's project of bringing that larger vision of wholeness into being.

⸻ ⸻ ⸻

Rock Island, Illinois. Fifteenth Avenue Christian Church. 2009. Members of the church, Helen and David Popp, sat comfortably at home watching TV. A news article on homeless youth caught their attention and their hearts. These children lived in their town. The very next day, Helen went to their pastor's office. "Can't we do something?" she asked. Pastor Dave Geenen thought they could. They contacted other churches, raised money and eventually located a building that became The Place 2B, providing a space, a meal, tutoring, and job training for homeless youth.[7]

Love in action. Extending the neighborhood.

The churches of Rock Island had moved from a mission of mercy to a movement for wholeness. They were no longer simply reaching out, loving God by loving neighbor and creating communities of God's love, as important as that is! They had started asking, "What can be done to stop homelessness among youth in the first place?" They had progressed beyond treating symptoms and were reaching for the cure. A larger vision of a city where young people are not homeless at all had captured this congregation. They were now ready to enlist in that project, to partner with God in healing a part of their world. They were ready to help bring into being God's intention for wholeness.

They were right in line with the trajectory that Jesus had set.

Shalom

When Jesus launched his ministry as described in Luke 4, he proclaimed release to captives, sight for the blind, and good news for the poor. He called for a completely different way of life—socially, politically, and personally—than he and his generation experienced under the domination of Rome. He proposed a radically transformed way of being together in the world. It was not a brand new vision. In part, he was drawing upon a rich biblical tradition of "shalom."

———◇◇◇——— ———◇◇◇——— ———◇◇◇———

Christmas cards know all about shalom.

A lion with a big curly mane (looking much less ferocious than lions in the wild) lies down beside a cute, wooly lamb. Other animals gather harmoniously around them in a "peaceable kingdom." Together they make a charming example of shalom, drawing from Isaiah's description of a domain of endless peace, justice, and righteousness:[8]

> The wolf shall live with the lamb,
>> the leopard shall lie down with the kid,
> the calf and the lion and the fatling together,
>> and a little child shall lead them.[9]

The poetry of the Psalms weighs in as well to describe a world of shalom. Psalm 85[10] says that when God dwells on the earth:

> Steadfast love and faithfulness will meet;
>> righteousness and peace will kiss each other.
> Faithfulness will spring up from the ground,
>> and righteousness will look down from the sky.

The Hebrew word *shalom* describes something about God's best vision for the earth. English translations often define it as "peace." In reality, however, shalom depicts a more complex notion. It comes from a root word that means "whole," as in "complete" or "safe," either personally or within society.[11] Shalom does not indicate a passive harmony or mere absence of conflict, as the word *peace* sometimes does. Shalom evokes a situation that is actively good, where the circumstances offer opportunities for individuals and communities to flourish.

Shalom implies that God did not intend life to be a zero-sum game where one person moves forward only at another's expense. In the biblical notion of shalom, creation's natural abundance provides enough for all to thrive. The world's nations stream to the light of God,[12] where all experience shalom. A good translation for shalom is "wholeness."

———∿∿∾— ———∿∿∾— ——∿∿∾—

The opening scene of the Bible itself shows God weaving wholeness into the original fabric of creation.

The curtain opens. Immediately, God is at work. "In the beginning" God creates heavens and earth—light, vegetation, and animals—and finally two human beings, the original cosmic parents. In the poetry of the creation accounts,[13] all human beings descend from these two. These very first chapters in the Bible establish the basic assumption for all that follows. Humanity is a single family. The distinctions of race, language, and culture—and the all too frequent attendant dysfunction—come later.

In God's original intention, humanity is undivided. Whole.

———∿∿∾— ——∿∿∾— ——∿∿∾—

A vision of wholeness emerges repeatedly throughout scripture. The prophets who painted the vision of shalom were not blind to a broken world in need of repentance and repair. They had hope in spite of the world's fragmentation. In contemporary times, as well, the world hopes for such wholeness. We see it expressed at least every four years.

———∿∿∾— ——∿∿∾— ——∿∿∾—

When the Olympic athletes move into the stadium on the closing night of the Olympics, they celebrate. Days of competition and medals, courage and heartbreak are behind them—magnificent accomplishments in sport. The mood of the ceremony has changed from the Olympians' first appearance seventeen days earlier.

The first night's pageantry includes the precisely scripted entry of athletes according to nationality. Uniquely designed uniforms distinguish each country's team. The last night presents a different scene. Now the athletes cross the threshold into the stadium as teams mixed, some wearing each other's hats, arms around each other. As the cameras pan the arena floor, the colors of their uniforms blend into random bursts and patterns of color marking new friendships. The image differs markedly from the carefully orchestrated pallet that helps identify each separate country on the first night. The appealing lightness in atmosphere contrasts with the ponderous first night. Celebration fills the air.

The closing ceremony also expresses the world's hope for peace and unity among the nations. It represents a vision of wholeness.

—∿— —∿— —∿—

The biblical prophets shared a hope for a repaired, healed world. They believed that by God's power working through God's people, the world can and will mend. Isaiah declares:

> The LORD has anointed me;
> he has sent me to bring good news to the oppressed,
>   to bind up the brokenhearted,
> to proclaim liberty to the captives,
>   and release to the prisoners;
> to proclaim the year of the LORD's favor,...
>   to comfort all who mourn.[14]

Jesus intentionally uses Isaiah's words to announce his ministry. The world is broken and sick, but God is at work to heal and restore. God is at work through those who love God to heal and restore a fragmented world to wholeness.

—∿— —∿— —∿—

A similar vision of wholeness emerges in the Christian story of the birth of the church.

Jesus has recently met his death. The disciples grieve deeply. Even so, they sense his presence, alive and well. Each one can report an encounter with their resurrected teacher. Still, they fear that their life with Jesus is over. They are concerned that they, like Jesus, might face arrest, perhaps even death, as his followers. On this day, they gather anxiously in a room in Jerusalem to pray. Outside, the Festival of Weeks, called Pentecost, has brought people into the city from all over the world, to offer their first fruits at the temple.

All at once, a sense of power and possibility overtakes the disciples and drives out their worry. They jump up and run into the street, talking to anyone who will listen. To the astonishment of all involved, everyone in this international crowd can understand them, no matter their mother tongue! As the throng grows larger, one of the disciples, Peter, takes advantage of the opportunity to explain what is going on.

Everyone has a chance to start all over again for a better life, he tells them—no matter what language you speak or where you are from; no matter what your economic class is or what you have done in your life. Here! Now! You can have a new beginning. God loves you, just as Jesus said.

Three thousand people joined with the original disciples that day. They formed a new community connecting people who normally were divided against each other.

They tried to emulate and expand on what Jesus had lived with his disciples. Though of varied backgrounds, they sought to come together as one. In some cases, they shared residences and resources. Gathering at table together regularly, they learned to sit next to whomever. Their understanding grew that no one deserved less of God's mercy than another. They, too, felt Jesus' spirit among them, alive, strengthening them for their new way of life as the leading edge of wholeness restored. The church was born.

Sometimes the early church lived its vision well. In fact, it was their effort to live into the wholeness of God's peaceable kingdom that would ultimately become the reason that Christianity spread worldwide.

⟨⟨⟨ ⟨⟨⟨ ⟨⟨⟨

By the fourth century, Christians were well established in many cities of the Mediterranean. The heady, egalitarian days of the earliest church had long since dissipated. Still, the leaders remembered Jesus' message of love. They knew to love God by loving their neighbors, extending the neighborhood beyond the cozy boundaries of their own kin and class. Their sense of call to love-in-action caused them to care for the poor in the cities. The bishops themselves had hands-on involvement.

Emperor Constantine noticed. The Empire marked a definitive turn toward Christianity when he and the eastern emperor Licinius issued the Edict of Milan in 313. Constantine favored the church, supported it financially, and encouraged the expansion of Christianity, partly because he saw how effective the Christian bishops were in caring for the poor and the sick. In that sense it was a political calculation. This Christianity that tended so well to the poor could help keep the peace among the masses. The bishops' record of reaching out in love to the poor had a hand in contributing to Christianity becoming the religion of Constantine.[15] By the end of the century, it had become the religion of the Empire.[16]

In this was good news: on the wings of empire, the word flew. The church spread to the known ends of the earth.

The bad news: empire ultimately cages its birds.

———————

The bishops in the early Constantine era "got it." They were doing what the church is supposed to do. Loving God is not just about reaching out to a first ring of neighbors; it is about extending the neighborhood progressively until the world changes into a place of well being for all God's children. The bishops were living out in real time Jesus' vision of shalom, of wholeness. They were offering mercy, bringing care, and demonstrating God's vision of the world by modeling it themselves. As church they were showing already what the whole world could be like eventually: a world where everyone had a chance to flourish.

Only, it was supposed to be God's kingdom they were representing, not the kingdom of Constantine or Theodosius.

Throughout history, it has proven difficult to disentangle God's work from the king's work. The dreadful record shows just how much the intended character of the church can be distorted by its captivity to empire. The church, to its shame, has legitimized European colonialism, North American slavery, Nazism, and apartheid. Less dramatically, but no less importantly, the church today participates in twenty-first–century North American structures of white privilege and economic power. So continues the mis-shaping of the church's character as a foretaste of God's intended wholeness. Silence in the face of injustice or active support of destructive ideologies—either one—compromises the character of the church born on Pentecost.

As sign of a common table where all are welcome and loved, as a foretaste of God's reign of wholeness, the church is called to do better.

The Reign of God

Fortunately, even in eras where much of the church has lost its way, a remnant has continued to call and act for wholeness. The great early Christian teacher, Paul, said once, "In past generations...[God] has not left himself without a witness..."[17] Even in terrible times, simple actions of the faithful stand as a promise for wholeness against the powers of the world. Sometimes the simplest thing can make all the difference.

—◦◦◦◦— —◦◦◦◦— —◦◦◦◦—

At first just a few people started chipping away at the concrete with hand tools. That day in 1989 they walked right up to the Berlin Wall in the sight of armed guards. Unbelievably, no one stopped these daring souls. In that era before social media, somehow other people appeared out of nowhere to help. Within days, after forty painful years, the wall came down.

The groundwork for that surge of people ready to tear down the wall came in part due to a movement among East German Christians.[18] For eight years people had been rendezvousing at churches on a certain night of the week. After gathering, they would exit the building and march around the town square, singing Christian songs, and calling out for freedom. That they called for freedom from NATO presence as well as Soviet presence probably helps explain the restraint of the police. They let the protests continue.

A generation into Cold War reality, in this basically atheist culture, people began to see the church as a place to register their democratic will. People mattered there. The marches became places where many young East Germans heard for the first time the Christian message of God's love for all people. They heard it through the words of the simple songs they learned marching around the square.[19]

The situation came to a head on October 8, 1989, in Leipzig. The numbers in the marches were swelling. The press was on hand, soldiers at the ready. Everyone participating felt certain that this evening would end in a confrontation. But to the surprise of all, the East German officials, in close contact with Moscow, did not call on the military to act. The people marched undeterred. One month later the wall came down. According to Elizabeth Pond of the *Christian Science Monitor,* "East German parliamentary Speaker

Horst Sindermann famously admitted later, 'We were ready for everything—everything except candles and prayers.'"[20]

When Christians are doing their job, living as if God's reign of wholeness already extends to all, even empires need to pay attention.

———

In Jesus' case, catching the attention of the Roman Empire yielded mixed results.

———

The people in the community who heard Jesus's words, "The Spirit of the Lord is upon me...to bring good news to the poor... to proclaim release to the captives...," would have been justified in receiving his words with some skepticism. It's all well and good to read the Bible, they might have thought. However, some things are surely meant to be taken spiritually. And they would have had a point. Prophetic passages such as the one Jesus read imply that the people have power to act, that they are free to behave as God and the prophets describe. In Jesus' time, however, the facts on the ground did not support free choice or action on the part of the people.

In those days, the emperor of Rome had full, divinely appointed authority. Surrounded by a small band of loyal and powerful courtiers, he controlled a vast army who made sure he got his way. Puppet leaders ruled the provinces and countries under the emperor's power. Their main job was to keep order and to extract money and resources in order to support the lavish lifestyles of the rich, as well as to fund the Empire's wars of expansion.

The peasants in the conquered areas, including Jesus' homeland, made up the vast majority of the population. In spite of their numbers, however, they did not have rights or freedom in the way that North American citizens would expect today. They lived under the watchful eye of Rome in the form of soldiers and tax collectors.

Thus, when Jesus started reading the prophet's words as though he meant it, people shifted uncomfortably in their seats. They shook their heads. They rolled their eyes.

Outside of his hometown, people started taking Jesus more seriously. His ministry of wholeness was not just political. It was personal, too. They liked that. He healed the sick. People who had suffered for years with dread diseases such as leprosy, so bad that no one would go near them, found new life when Jesus touched them. Young children, thought to have died, rose up from their beds at Jesus' word. Crowds began to gather whenever Jesus passed through.

He also offered words of forgiveness. This generated more controversy. "Who is he to forgive sin?" people would ask— especially religious leaders. Yet, his words and touch healed persons from guilt, restored them to community, gave them the chance to begin again. The mending of brokenness through forgiveness had even more impact than the physical cures that first drew the crowds. Healing illness, putting fragmented communities back together—it all pointed toward wholeness both for the person and for society.

Jesus talked about this healing and restoration and new beginning as the "reign[21] of God." That is where the trouble began.

––––§§§–––– ––––§§§–––– ––––§§§––––

Jesus leads the disciples up the mountain, away from the crowds, for some advanced tutoring. He starts to teach them about the blessings of life that come to his followers.[22] Some of these "blessings" are pretty easy to understand and accept. "Blessed are the poor in spirit…" Yes, that sounds like the humility it takes to serve the needs of others, to engage in self-giving agape love. "Blessed are the pure in heart…" That, too, makes sense for the "love God, love neighbor" crowd.

Other blessings accrue to the love-in-action modality. "Blessed are the merciful…[and] those who hunger and thirst for righteousness."

It starts to get a little dicey after that, however. "Blessed are those who are persecuted for righteousness' sake…[or] revile[d]" for the sake of Jesus.

Did he say persecuted? Reviled? What is going on here?

To comprehend, we have to dig deeper into the reality of the Roman Empire. Remember: Rome controls the world: politics, economics, the military. You can almost hear the boots marching. All of it benefits Rome's elite few at the expense of the many.

In those days, the people address the Roman emperor as "Son of God," "Savior of the World". Messengers' reporting to the people about the emperor and his new conquests is called the "evangel," the "gospel." "Praise the Lord!" comes frequently from the lips of the people, but when they say it, they mean to praise Caesar. "The Kingdom" refers to Rome. To think anything else is disloyal. To say it out loud is treason.

No wonder Jesus goes up on the mountain for this talk with the disciples. His words bring an obvious and dangerous contrast to the empire of Caesar. Jesus' "reign of God" borrowed on familiar phrases from Caesar's world and turned them downside up. To even suggest the possibility of a kingdom other than Caesar's was to take a big risk. But Jesus went farther than that. He claimed God's kingdom deserved full allegiance.

"Blessed are the poor in spirit [not the high and mighty], for theirs is the kingdom of heaven," he said. Jesus has here introduced the new kingdom that is not Rome.

"Blessed are the pure in heart, for they will see God,...[and] the peacemakers, for they will be called children of God." Jesus has now turned the whole known world order upside down. Random people in Rome, especially peasants, are not supposed to see God. They are definitely not considered children of God.

Jesus uses the words of the Roman Empire against itself. God's will is known through Jesus, not through the emperor. In Jesus' "gospel," God's blessings extend to all the people, not just the few.

No wonder he eventually had to mention "persecution" and "reviling." Jesus' words are "put your life on the line" words. He does not want his disciples to keep this gospel, this news, to themselves for their own personal comfort. He wants them to spread the word, to mix it through all dimensions of life like a pinch of life-giving salt in a meal.[23]

He wants them to go public with the news of God's reign, like light, so everyone can see, so everyone can be part of it. As God's way of doing things takes over, all can experience the wholeness envisioned by God in creation, proclaimed by the prophets, modeled by Jesus in his dealings with the crowds.

Unfortunately for Jesus, to suggest any empire, kingdom, or reign other than that of Rome amounted to sedition. No wonder he, and those early Christians, ended up in so much trouble.

The teachings up on the mountain were only the beginning of his teaching. "The Reign of God is near," he said. "It is among you, at hand, now."[24] He told simple stories that made it seem real, that showed how even one person or small group of people could make a difference. God's Empire is like a mustard seed, he said: so small you can hardly see it, but when it grows, it becomes a large tree.[25] It is like a bit of yeast a woman puts into a loaf of bread. That little starter causes the whole loaf to rise.[26]

Jesus' stories described life in God's reign. The tale of the good Samaritan, already mentioned in chapter 1, portrayed a world resembling a neighborhood in which people show mercy to whoever has need. Elsewhere Jesus explained that those who feed the hungry, clothe the naked, or visit the sick and imprisoned are living as good citizens in God's empire.[27] He was emphatic, as reported in the book of John, that his followers are called to love one another, even to the point of laying down their lives for each other.[28]

Jesus' acts and words, and the world he describes, are a call to "shalom," to wholeness, to an active, self-giving way of life that puts the well-being of the other first. People who meet Jesus are called to change from self-centered to other-oriented in their way of life.

He was not only calling for individual acts of courage, however. All of his activities and preaching pointed to whole communities transformed on the way to restoring the world to God's original vision of wholeness. With his near last words, "Go therefore and make disciples of all nations...,"[29] Jesus called his followers to change the world by offering healing and repair that crossed the lines of national, political entities. He was calling for a peace that comes from bringing the broken pieces back together. He was calling for unity, justice, and peace—for a world made whole.

And how is the world supposed to be made whole?

It starts close to home. In small increments, Jesus' followers reach out across barriers with acts of love, expanding the neighborhood. "You give them something to eat,"[30] said Jesus. "The reign of God is among you." But those small beginnings engage the process of changing the world. "Go therefore and make disciples of all nations,... teaching them to obey everything that I have commanded you."

From the earliest Christians sharing their possessions, to the bishops seeing to it that the hungry were fed, to standing with those struggling for freedom, to building houses on a no-man's land between separated peoples, to founding a shelter for homeless teens, Jesus' followers, in the spirit of Pentecost, blur human-made boundaries. They build a world of wholeness by starting to live as if it already is.

～◦⁓ ～◦⁓ ～◦⁓

Jesus crossed the known boundaries of his time—gender, age, politics, health, economic status, culture, religion—in his witness for wholeness. In following his footsteps, some of the boundaries that we have to overcome are cultural, their roots so deeply buried that we cannot always see them.

In the United State, race is one of those boundaries.

Facing the Boundaries

It was an honor to be selected.

The push was on to have congregations select "youth voting representatives" to the every-other-year Indiana Disciples Regional Assembly. A couple of adults always went from each church, but it was rare to select a young person. In the late 1960s and early 1970s, with the youth movement in full swing, more age diversity was encouraged. My congregation complied and chose...me.

A certain sermon stands out in my memory, delivered by a young African American minister. A fiery preacher, the Rev. Tom Benjamin took full advantage of the opportunity to lay a challenge before the crowd of mostly white Hoosier Disciples. "If you're born in America," he said, "you're shaped by racism, like it or not. Intended or not, if you're white, you cannot help but be a racist. In this culture, with our history, there's no learning any other way to be."

Stunned by his uncompromising word, I nevertheless sensed the truth of it. In my home neighborhood, white families were moving into outer suburbs ringing the city. My parents, by moving the other direction, into that neighborhood, had signaled their intention to live in an integrated setting.

Volatility marked those years in the United States shortly after the assassination of Dr. Martin Luther King Jr. Court-ordered busing and school desegregation were also under way. Against the mood of the day, the school board tried to shut down our interracial high school. We students marched on their meeting to "Save Our School!" We did save it...for a few more years.

I would have hated to lose my high school. Especially the Madrigal Singers, one of the smaller school choirs. I sang alto. In keeping with our classical repertoire, the young men wore tuxes; the young women long dresses of Shortridge blue. We felt so elegant... though didn't always act it.

After concerts we would go out, often for cheesecake, at a little restaurant near the school. Its medieval décor provided a great backdrop for our attire. We often fell into an encore performance of our music. Pity the poor customers who just wanted a quiet, late-night coffee.

One evening, on the way home, two carloads of Madrigals were each trying to nose ahead of the other driving down the four-lane city street. The accelerating speed attracted the notice of a watchful police officer. He pulled us over, a good thing.

Approaching our car, he looked in, then did a double take, his face contorted in a grimace of disgust. He let us know that black and white young people mixing together as friends did not suit his sense of how things should be.

Sitting with church people in that regional assembly worship service, I recognized what Pastor Benjamin was talking about. Sometimes the racism is personal, direct, and mean. In the United States we are also shaped less obviously (at least to white people) by the distorted history and reality of racial prejudice and the resulting injustices we have all inherited. Before Pastor Benjamin's sermon, I had not been familiar with the term "systemic racism." I could see its meaning, however. To seek God's wholeness related to race is to seek an end to both personal and systemic bias and the mismatched opportunities that result for too many people.

At the time of that regional assembly, I was not aware that our denomination had a long history of dealing with race, some of it positive. The story is told of Dr. A. Dale Fiers, first General Minister and President, in a meeting with Dallas Disciples sometime in the mid-Sixties.[31] The International Convention, as it was then called, was to take place there—a big deal for the local hosts who put money and hours of time into making it happen. The plan included an invitation to another fiery African American preacher by the name of the Rev. Dr. Martin Luther King Jr. to preach at the Dallas convention.

Tension mounted at the meeting when someone suggested that maybe Dallas wasn't the place for that particular preacher. Dr. Fiers was not tense. He looked at his associate seated nearby. "Which are the other cities that want this assembly?" he asked.

—————   —————   —————

Disciples minister James A. Garfield served as the only ordained clergyperson ever elected as President of the United States (however briefly). The *Washington Post*[32] has called his inaugural address the best statement on race by a United States president until Lyndon B. Johnson (another Disciple) spoke at the passage of the Voting Rights Act.

Statements are not enough, and Disciples have tried to do more. In 1970, in response to urban unrest, the church founded Reconciliation Ministry. This fund helps the church, locally and more broadly, engage in hands-on activities to cross the boundaries of racial prejudice and racism. Since the 1970s Disciples have undertaken hundreds of projects with Reconciliation funds. These projects seek to dismantle the boundaries of racism in an attempt to participate with God in restoring God's world of wholeness.

The Church talks about this kind of world-restoring work as doing justice. Love says I want for my neighbor, including my world neighbor, all that I want for myself. Justice says I am willing to contend with the unfair barriers that keep them from having it. The prophet Micah said, "What does the Lord require of you / but to do justice, and to love kindness, / and to walk humbly with your God?"[33] Seeking world-changing wholeness requires a passion for justice. It involves contending with the powers that be, as Jesus did.

Striving for wholeness requires seeking justice.

A Passion for Justice

The twelve congregations joining together to form a brand new organization in Kansas City included four from the Disciples.[34] They were each already involved in hands-on work to help their neighbor through various mercy ministries such as food pantries—a beautiful and necessary love-in-action kind of outreach. With the new organization, called the Metro Organization for Racial and Economic Equity ("More Squared" or "More²"), they wanted to go further. They wanted to help build toward a day when there were not so many hungry people to feed in the first place. They wanted to reach across every imaginable barrier. They wanted to help their city be more like God's vision of wholeness.

More² tackled their first major issue in the midst of a multimillion–dollar building boom going on in Kansas City. The churches had noticed a lack of inclusion of minorities and women in the workforce, even in the government funded projects that supposedly required it. Creating a conversation called the Jericho Table, More² decided to promote the creation of city ordinances to ensure minorities' and women's participation in those building projects. Their work helped the ordinances pass. Of particular significance, the legislation for the building of the brand new $250 million Icon Bridge (later called the Kit Bond Bridge) contained both provisions for minority hiring and $1.25 million for training women and minorities in the construction of the bridge.

A passion for justice within the Kansas City faith community led to more jobs, more women and men from all ethnic groups trained to do them, and fewer hungry people.

From that beginning, More² went on to address transportation issues, access to health care, creation of supermarkets in urban food deserts, and an education initiative to provide mentors and tutors to 10,000 students. Through More², now more than twenty churches are loving the God who first loved them by reaching across barriers to help meet their neighbors' need. They are also changing the larger situation by reducing such need in the first place. They are creating a zone more resembling wholeness in their part of the world. They are doing their part to extend God's vision of wholeness throughout the entire world.

More² takes its biblical mandate from Jesus' Luke 4 world-changing declaration, "The Spirit of the Lord…has anointed me / to bring good news to the poor."[35] They remember as well the words of the prophet Micah, "What does the LORD require of you / but to do justice, and to love kindness, / and to walk humbly with your God?"[36]

—⁓⁓— —⁓⁓— —⁓⁓—

Justice work, helping to make the world whole for all, requires passion, courage, and persistence, as well as the vision to work together. In a much-quoted fable, Donald B. Ardell[37] tells of a town located on a river. One day they notice a person drowning. They manage to rescue him. Unfortunately, he is not the only one. Every once in a while, and eventually more and more often, people come floating down the river in dire peril. The people of the town manage to save many, though not all. In order to improve their rate of rescue they install the most modern saving technology. The numbers of people coming down river grow. Eventually someone thinks to ask an obvious question—shouldn't we go up river to find out what is causing these people to be in the river in the first place? Unfortunately, they are too busy with their rescue efforts to seek an answer.

Going up river to seek the answer is the work of justice. Justice work assumes people do not have to go without, and communities do not have to be divided. Justice work figures out what is causing the fragmentation we live with every day and then does something about it.

—⁓⁓— —⁓⁓— —⁓⁓—

Not everyone is comfortable with the world-changing dimension of loving God and loving neighbor. The boundary line between church and political or social action should remain a bright, clear line, they assert. Let the church stick to its charity work.

Why should we not just stick to our own small devices? Because isolated acts of kindness or mercy are not enough to meet the need, nor enough to honor the reign of God.

—⁓⁓— —⁓⁓— —⁓⁓—

A well-organized, citywide hunger action network blesses the city of Indianapolis. All of the major hunger relief agencies, together with representatives of faith communities, gather regularly to pool resources and information and to lay out strategies toward the day when no person in Indianapolis goes hungry. In 2012, they figured they were really close; perhaps no more than 5000 people in the entire city could be counted as truly hungry.

Even in Indianapolis, a startling statistic sobers the mind. As with most major urban areas, absolutely all the volunteer and nonprofit efforts added together provide a mere 7 percent of all hunger relief in the city. All of the food pantries, all the soup kitchens, all the shelters, all the hands-on, heart-involved, love-thy-neighbor hunger-relief efforts take care of only 7 percent of Indianapolis hunger relief.

It is a very important 7 percent, but it is still 7 percent. The rest, the other 93 percent, is funded by all of the American people gathering together through federally funded programs such as school lunches and food stamps (SNAP).

Followers of Jesus need to notice our neighbor's need. We need to do something about it. And we also need to enlist the aid of many, many others as we show our love of God and love of neighbor. Part of the work in our democracy is to enlist legislators to make good laws, to respond to the need of members of our human family, neighbors that we do not even know, but neighbors nonetheless. As with Abraham so long ago,[38] attention to hungry neighbors serves a certain self-interest. "A hungry man is an angry man."[39] More importantly for Christians, hunger relief serves the purposes of bringing wholeness to a fragmented world.

—◦◦◦— —◦◦◦— —◦◦◦—

Jesus lived in a time of Roman oppression. Even so, he invited his followers to act as if their captivity had already given way to freedom, as if God had created a world with more than enough to go around. Jesus called his followers to extend mercy and kindness to others regardless of nation or clan. He urged them to be generous with their possessions and their community boundaries. He helped them to understand that the world belongs to God, who made it. He showed them that God is a God of love who desires justice, peace, unity—wholeness—for the whole human family.

People still catch the vision of a world beyond barriers today:

> *The church in California* with the ministry to the homeless, where the homeless themselves want to help change the world. They run a Saturday bicycle clinic on the church grounds, with spare parts donated by local shops. From scratch, these homeless mechanics build

bikes that give poor children of the neighborhood
their first sense of independence.

The church in Indianapolis, after shrinking to near extinction,
which has found new life in social action: advocating
for workers' rights and better public transportation;
but which especially attributes its current growth and
flourishing to its uncompromising welcome to gay,
lesbian, bisexual, and transgender persons.

The congregation in which a group of Montagnards from
the Vietnam high country (traditionally Christian),
now refugees in the United States, have found a home
in Charlotte, North Carolina. Some fifty or more are
members of the Church. In touch with their families
at home, they lead advocacy efforts now in the United
States against persecution in Vietnam.

U.S. Disciples who have been in partnership with Congolese
Disciples for generations, hearing the stories of the
long-lasting war in eastern Congo. They learn
of the minerals, such as coltan, fueling that war, and
of the devastating use of rape as a weapon. The
relationship leads to advocacy for sisters and brothers
a world away.

Martin Luther King Jr. said, "The arc of universe is long,
but bends toward justice."[40] He used to talk about the "Beloved
Community," another way of saying that, in a God's eye view of
earth, boundaries blur. Diversity exists, but not divisiveness. Barriers
that would hold some back while others are allowed to run forward
unobstructed fade away. Children do not want for food, and workers
receive their wages. Youth are not homeless. Wholeness prevails in
the reign of God.

When we think about Jesus feeding the 5000, all of them worthy
in his eyes; when we see him sitting with any and all at the table;
when we read in the last chapters of Bible about "the leaves of the
tree...for the healing of the nations";[41] we can begin to imagine a
world of justice and peace for all people regardless of race, economic
status, or religion. We see a world of wholeness. From the moment

we receive God's welcoming love, we embark on a journey leading us inexorably to work for that world.

QUESTIONS
Chapter 3

1. What are some of the ideas and opinions you've heard about the ecumenical movement? Nothing? Confusion? It's good and worth supporting? It's what Disciples do? What are ways that your church is involved in the ecumenical movement?

2. How does changing the word unity to wholeness (shalom) change the meaning of how separated Christians relate to one another and to the larger community?

3. What are some barriers you have noticed or experienced that block God's vision of wholeness from being realized? What makes people resist this vision?

4. How are churches in your community working together on behalf of wholeness?

5. What are other ways churches could provide wholeness for the community and the world? What are some ways you could promote wholeness?

4

Movement

A Movement for Wholeness

Minnie Vautren's feet are firmly planted, her arms spread wide in a blocking gesture. She intends that no one get past her. Her eyes behind the spectacles narrow in determination. Women and children peer out from behind her skirts in fear. The moment, represented in sculpture at the Nanjing Massacre Memorial, captures the reason Minnie Vautren, Disciples missionary teacher from the United States, lives in memory as the Goddess of Nanjing.[1]

In 1937, World War II came early to the then capital of China with mass killings and brutal rape. As the Japanese imperial Army laid siege, most who could fled. Among those who stayed was a small group of foreigners, including American Disciples missionaries. They joined together with other expatriates to form a safe zone at several of the schools and embassies. Protected by nothing other than naked courage and an American flag, they blocked doorways, denying entrance against armed military. The teachers could have chosen to leave. By staying, they saved hundreds of thousands of women and children from rape, murder, and slavery.

These Westerners stood with friends and colleagues of their adopted country, running interference with the soldiers when they could have run back home. In so doing, they expressed God's love as

Jesus lived it among humanity. Missionary solidarity in WWII China meant life itself to an astonishing number of people.

God loves the world and wants it to be whole. When we love God back by loving each other we become part of a movement for wholeness. We participate with God in remaking a world of justice and peace. One or two people can make a huge difference, even now.

Urgency for a World Made New

The world could definitely stand to have a makeover. In the early twenty-first century, division reigns more than ever in a world far from whole. Oil, land, and religion pit nations against each other, ultimately threatening the well being of all. Sadly, World War II stands as only the first in a succession of wars following "the war to end all wars."

Countries experience division within their borders as well. In the United States, the lines demarcating "red states" and "blue states," liberal and conservative, rich and poor, young and old, black and white stay stubbornly bright. In certain other countries sectarian violence takes on legendary proportions. Even the church all too often participates in the divisive behavior. "Red pews" and "blue pews," patterned after the political in-fighting of a nation, take up residence in the most sacred of spaces.

Such division seems particularly out of place in an era of extraordinary communication.

———————— ———————— ————————

In the late 1970s, I lived and worked as a global mission intern[2] in Democratic Republic of Congo (then Zaire.) To communicate with my parents, I, like everyone in the day, wrote longhand on blue airmail stationery. Letters took weeks to get home. The replies, arriving in Congo with its not very dependable infrastructure, could take weeks to reach me.

In 2008, thirty years later, my husband and I visited the country again. This time, we sat under mosquito netting in the depths of the tropical rain forest and talked directly with our children in Indianapolis *on the phone* in real time!

———————— ———————— ————————

The mind-blowing technological advances of the twentieth and twenty-first centuries give new truth to the old wisdom, "It's a small world." Digital communication makes it possible to cross every kind of boundary as never before, from national frontiers to time zones to the International Dateline. And yet, as technology expands the global neighborhood, we have more trouble than ever communicating with each other. Though Earth seems "smaller," the journey toward a remade world of wholeness grows longer.

Division serves not only to keep us separated from each other; it also masks or even encourages unequal access by different groups to the world's resources. Globally, more than one billion people live in extreme poverty—that is, on less than $1.25 a day.[3] When was the last time you tried to get a cup of coffee for a dollar? Even in the world's very richest country, nearly 50 million people live in poverty.[4] In many parts of the world, the gap between the haves and the have not's grows wider.

Those on the wrong side of whatever the dividing line may be (the poor, children and women, people of color, inhabitants of the global south), suffer disproportionately. The very cell phone helping me to communicate from Congo to Indianapolis requires coltan, a metallic ore, to function. Ironically, most of the world's coltan comes from Congo. Until recent legislation was passed,[5] it was most often gained illegally in a brutal war in eastern Congo involving multiple nations and militia. The war is fueled by people wanting a share of the profits, most of which go to transnational corporations in a chillingly ironic play on how "wholeness" does benefit those who can pull it off.[6]

The planet itself is in peril as the global economic machine powers on. Those who receive the biggest benefits from the overuse of fossil fuels are distanced from the consequences. The United States and Canada barely notice as faraway Congolese and Amazon rain forests, the lungs of the earth, shrink and become endangered. The alarm sounded by the atmosphere's over-rich CO_2 content is not yet heard in the faraway centers of decision-making power.

Meanwhile, adding to the sense of vulnerability, the cult of individualism already familiar in the Western world takes on new and frightening possibilities. Technological advances can put great power into the hands of isolated individuals, making us all more susceptible to danger from the individual holding either a gun or a cellphone ignition. Thomas Friedman, in his book *The World Is Flat,* suggests that we describe this rapidly changing world as "flat": a leveled playing field for the technologically savvy. With electronic information and communication winning out over print, even transnational corporations have to reckon with loose networks of isolated individuals who can log onto computers or cell phones to resource each other out of anonymous stores of information and new processes of information manipulation.[7]

The wake of a global economy forging ahead overtakes those outside the digitized, computerized world of technology. Those who do not yet participate in the "flat" communications landscape become the victims of war, raids on natural resources, human trafficking, and forced migration. They need advocacy, solidarity, and justice. The global, flat, clashing world increases the urgency for a world made new. It calls out to good Samaritans who would join together in a movement for wholeness to change the world through acts of love and expanding the neighborhood.

However, not everybody looks ahead to find the answer.

Many voices insist that we should begin our journey toward wholeness by retracing our steps: "Give me that old-time religion"; "Return to traditional values"; "What is this generation coming to?"

The desire to turn back the clock even crosses the faith line. Reza Aslan suggests that part of the upheaval in the Muslim world can be understood as an internal struggle of old against new, as Islam, like Christianity, struggles to find rebirth into the twenty-first century.[8]

We simply cannot go back. In the first place, the past did not have the answers either. Furthermore, our smaller world through technology presents us with genuinely new challenges. We live closer to our diverse global neighbors. Face to face with them, we recognize the need to share resources more broadly. As we share more fully in experience and conversation with our neighbors, we begin to know why some of the old answers do not work. What seems simple and obvious from within the conceptual confines of a particular cultural worldview, often presents as neither simple nor obvious when viewed from another perspective.

—⎯⎯⎯⎯   —⎯⎯⎯⎯   —⎯⎯⎯⎯

The Pacific Islander woman sitting there with us in our small circle of chairs riveted our attention. The ninth Assembly of the World Council of Churches, in Porto Alegre, Brazil, began each day with Bible study. An Australian delegate led our group, including people from the United States, Europe, Asia, and Africa. We listened to this woman describe the sea level creeping up on her island home. She did not mean just her house. Her whole island is being swallowed by water. Her homeland is now identified as one of the first places that will disappear, along with its inhabitants and culture, as the oceans rise from global warming.

That very day at lunch my husband sat with a Malaysian delegate to the assembly. This pastor reported in a shaking voice that because the United States is known as a Christian nation, American foreign policy decisions routinely put his own life at risk. He, too, is a Christian. Whenever the United States makes a "national security" decision that endangers the national security of his country, guards have to be posted around Christian churches and people. Christians in predominantly Muslim countries around the world are often associated with the Western, Christian "enemy." Decisions made on one side of the globe affect the other.

At that same World Council of Churches meeting, Pastor Clement Mputu, Vice President of the Disciples of Christ in Congo, looked straight into my eyes. Anguish tightened his face as he told me about the 6 million people who have died in the Congo war. *Six million.* "Doesn't anybody even care?" he asked. And then he stopped, waiting for an answer.

—⎯⎯⎯⎯   —⎯⎯⎯⎯   —⎯⎯⎯⎯

When the world is small enough to know personally the people affected by our decisions, life gets more complicated. Actually meeting these people, brothers and sisters in Christ, requires more from us. The world shrinks in size, but the neighborhood expands.

More people come into view. We begin to see with our own eyes the neighbors by the side of the road.

The Lay of the Land

We are not the first ever to experience a new situation requiring new responsibilities.

<hr />

As the era of industrialism reached full flower, poverty, too, took root. In the cities, far from tillable land and extended families, want had risen to a new level. Six Disciples women in St. Louis met to pray. They agonized especially about widows and orphans without means to provide for themselves. As the women talked, an idea began to take shape. What if they and their churches banded together and organized a home? They imagined providing safe shelter to widows and orphans in that new industrialized urban landscape. The effort of these six women led to scores of other benevolent ministries taking shape among Disciples for more than a hundred years. Many of them still exist today.[9]

The St. Louis women may have been familiar with the story of Abram and Sarai.

<hr />

Abram was no spring chicken. The biblical book of Genesis[10] tells us that Abram had reached age 75, an age seemingly more suited for retirement than for new adventures, when God called him with his wife, Sarai, to go to a "land that I will show you." They did not have a map, a GPS, or a known destination. (I myself usually like to travel with all three in hand!) At God's call Abram and Sarai went anyway. They set off to a new land as yet unknown, following a trail as yet uncharted.

It took a while, but God eventually did show them to a land and a future.

The truth is, the way forward in our time involves working our way through some unfamiliar territory with some little known traveling companions. Nevertheless, in the early twenty-first century the basic contours of the landscape are at least beginning to appear.

Technological change emerges as a significant characteristic going forward. It brings with it a different way of processing information and considerably more information than ever before. Increased knowledge does not necessarily mean the wisdom to understand what we are learning. It does, however, help bring a broader picture into view as more perspectives enter into the conversation.

The global diversity we experience through improved communication and transportation also emerges as part of the local landscape on our twenty-first–century journey.

In the year 2012, no single majority racial-ethnic group predominated among children born in the United States.[11] For the first time in United States history, white babies made up less than half the births that year. It has never happened before that a generation of United States residents would experience no numerical racial majority.

Growing racial-ethnic diversity means that different cultures and language groups come into contact in ways that often have been experienced only in the largest cities or at global meetings. It also means that for the first time white Americans need to learn to move comfortably in more than one culture, become familiar with more than one language, and understand the relativity of their own cultural norms.

Diversity in our time extends beyond race and ethnicity. In the early twenty-first century, more generations of adults rub shoulders than ever before in history.

Our graduate student daughter announced that she would be writing her American Religious History dissertation on the Equal Rights Amendment of the 1970s. Her father expressed surprise. "Honey, that's not history. It's journalism! I lived that stuff! And it wasn't all that long ago!"

Our daughter rolled her eyes just a little bit. "Daddy, when you study the 1970s, it's history!"

━∿∿━ ━∿∿━ ━∿∿━

Multiple generations, whose worldviews are shaped by different historical moments, who listen to different kinds of music, who have different patterns of behavior and morality, are all trying to get along and build together a society. In the twenty-first century, diverse perspectives, needs, and desires compete with each other and call for a new cultural narrative that makes room for all.

Phyllis Tickle describes this time as a once-every-500-year turnover of the world as we know it.[12] She likens it to the Protestant Reformation. Back then, the 500-year total turn happened in great part because Gutenberg's printing press opened new worlds of possibility. Today the digital revolution extends our world much further, even while it shakes our foundation.

No wonder we feel grief, anger, and fear. With traditional ways of life jeopardized, many experience an enormous sense of loss. And yet we must move forward. Fortunately, some of our familiar belongings can go with us.

Beginning the Journey

Moving to a new house can be quite an experience for a family. After being in one place for a number of years, packing up for a new address reveals just how much a few people can acquire in a surprisingly short period of time. Relocation may involve a yard sale, trips to drop off clothes at the thrift shop, and multiple decisions to relinquish items that should have been disposed of long ago.

But some items simply must go along to the new home. Being at home means holding the favorite coffee cup every morning, seeing the familiar picture hung above the couch, draping grandma's quilt over the bed.

In one of the greatest moves of all time, as recorded in the Bible, the people of Israel escaped from slavery in Egypt and headed toward a new land to make a new home.[13] They had left in haste with an army on their tail and could take with them only what they could carry. Their leader Moses made sure, however, to take along the bones of their patriarch Joseph.[14] Those bones would be buried in their proper place, at the end of the journey.

An odd choice of item to take, perhaps, except that those bones symbolized both where they had been and where they were going. Joseph had come as a slave to Egypt, but, because God was with him he became the agent of his family's survival when there was famine in the land of Canaan and they were threatened with poverty and starvation. In Egypt, they found food, security, and life. In Egypt, they also fell into slavery. Now, with Moses leading, they headed back to Canaan, which had apparently become a "land flowing with milk and honey."[15] They took with them the bones of the first victim and most powerful agent of their exile as a reminder of the good times and the bad. Joseph's bones represented the identity of the people as well as God's promise to get them home.

Travelers in our time too, who would participate in a movement for wholeness are journeying toward to a new "place" in history's landscape. They have to ask: What do we leave behind in order to travel more lightly and unencumbered for the journey? Equally important is: What do we take with us?

We do not know all of the answers. Yet, just as Moses took Joseph's bones, we go forward with our love for God, our love of neighbor, and our desire to move at God's call toward wholeness. These define us as followers of Christ.

Our broken and fragmented world needs to know this God of love and that this God's people intend to act to make a difference.

As we travel through this new territory, we start to become familiar with the lay of the land. We also get to know our traveling companions better, and we discover that our new companions bring not only challenge but also blessing.

The delegation putt-putts up the Congo River in two large dug-out canoes, lashed together, propelled by a small outboard motor. In the middle of those canoes, two ministers engage in deep conversation. "Regional ministers," their charge is to guide and resource congregations in a certain geographical area. The one from Indiana does his work by getting in his car and driving from church to church on paved highways. He sleeps in his bed most nights. The one from Mbandaka sets off on his rounds in a dug-out canoe, tramps on foot for days through the rain forest, and sleeps on the ground in order to tend his charges.

But as Rev. Spleth and Rev. Ilumbe share their stories, barely speaking the same language even, they nevertheless understand each other perfectly. They do the same work in guiding churches. They experience the same trials tending to the needs of diverse congregations and pastors and pastors' families. They learn from each other, not just about their work, but also about the expanded world each of them is beginning to cherish through the other.

The partnership of these two regions, one in North America, one in Africa, involves a kind of spiritual hospitality—opening to each other, learning to accept and love each other, warts and all. It involves acknowledging the painful differences of shocking material imbalance, of devastating historical wrongs, of divergent theology. And yet these partners discover and celebrate a deeper unity in their shared life in Christ Jesus.

The journey forward takes us through new territory with new companions who often bring to our attention confusing new realities. And yet through them we begin to live right now as if we are already one human family: one large neighborhood expanding in the name of a God of love.

Yes, the trek leads uphill much of the time. The world is in dire straits. The task looms large. And, yes, the world resists wholeness.

But we have already seen that one or a handful of people can spark a movement that matters. The early bishops in the Roman Empire caught the eye of the emperor; the ecumenical movement made possible a table of peace; church people helped bring down the Berlin Wall; a dream of housing for all made Habitat for Humanity a worldwide phenomenon.

One person can make a difference. When we join together, it matters even more.

Movement

On the evening of December 1, 1955, in Montgomery, Alabama, Rosa Parks took a seat on a bus. She was tired from a long day's work, and more than tired of a lifetime of legal double standards skewed against her and other African Americans. What happened next, her refusal to give her seat to a white man, stands as an iconic American act of individual resistance to a social wrong. Mrs. Parks' courage in the moment to insist on her human rights pitted one African American woman against the white man, a uniformed bus driver, and a bus full of people; against police officers who would arrest her; and against a system that held her to be of less value than her white co-bus-rider. This act of heroism helped turn the tide against a blatant system of racist laws in the United States. We rightfully lift up Mrs. Parks as a hero and celebrate the difference one person can make.

We take nothing away from her act of courage by observing also that Mrs. Parks was not alone. She belonged to a movement just getting underway.[16] Her fateful refusal did not amount to a rash, spur-of-the-moment decision. Rosa Parks, like others of her generation, had been preparing for the moment when providence or coincidence would offer the opportunity to make a "stand." Trained in nonviolent resistance at the Highlander Folk School, when the moment presented itself she knew what to do. Her connections, in the movement certainly, but also in the larger community and in her church meant that her action did not begin and end with herself.

During and after her arrest, brief incarceration, and trial, she was supported by a network of friends and a church family who valued her, not only as a child of God, but as a person of integrity and faith. That Rosa Parks had confronted the system in this way spread through her community of support, and the movement which had prepared her gained strength through her arrest in a way that it had not through the arrests of others before her.

Within days, the Montgomery Bus boycott had been organized and successfully launched. A new-to-the-scene twenty-six-year-old pastor, named the Rev. Dr. Martin Luther King Jr., had been recruited as leader among the churches. History as we know it was unfolding.

—————— —————— ——————

Rosa Parks was ready. She was one and many. What do we need to do to participate in God's movement for wholeness?

It takes some preparation. The enormity of the task itself can overwhelm to the point of paralysis. The horizon, in its beauty, can seem far away and impossible to reach. It can seem too big to even try.

Preparation includes learning to take it in bite-sized pieces. We start where we are. We begin in our own neighborhood.

In the familiar story, a young person walks along the beach. The tide has washed in starfish as far as the eye can see and left them stranded. The young person picks a few of them up and throws them, one by one, back into the life-giving water. A passerby asks, "What good do you think you are doing? There are so many and you are saving so few."

The young person answers, "It matters to each one of those few." [17]

We take the first step. We can accept the challenge to believe that we are part of something that makes a difference in the world and get started. The job may seem too big. We may feel too small. But if not us, who? The often-repeated saying bears truth: "We are the ones we've been waiting for."

When I preached at President Obama's inauguration, I noted that in troubled times we may find ourselves instinctively choosing between fight or flight. Ultimately, the buck often stops at the President's desk. As I said to the President that day, "Tag, you're it."

But the truth really is, "Tag, we're all it." Our voices can speak up to say, "It can be different." The world will be different when we reach out to embrace our neighbors. We have seen one person make a difference. We can follow that lead. Indeed, Disciples women in 2009 took the motto, "Tag, you're it," and used it as a motivating cry to make a difference in their own communities. They took resistance to human trafficking as their particular cause. Freeing women in Indianapolis, trafficked in for the Super Bowl, stands among the achievements in part through their efforts.

Our motivation for change begins where we are. Each one of us starts in our own space—realizing that our space is also a global space: our neighborhood is as big as the world. In Illinois, it began with backpacks. In Indiana it began with Spanish language Bibles. In

Nanjing it began by teachers standing their ground. Mrs. Parks took a strategic seat on the bus. Disciples women joined a movement to set twenty-first–century captives free.

Jesus said, "The reign of God is at hand. It is among you." We begin by each one of us doing our part.

One by one, it adds up. Together we make a difference.

⚞〰〰〰⚟

We were on the very southern tip of India. The women of the town greeted us with trays of burning incense and bowls of scented water bearing floating flowers. Not too many years earlier a tsunami had wiped this area clear of people, houses, and boats. On this day we had gathered to dedicate new homes. We launched new boats. We participated in the people's joy.

This village had almost been missed. In the rush to help, the NGO's had somehow passed this one by. But Disciples and United Church of Christ Global Ministries had come alongside them. We had helped them rebuild, acquire new boats, and give them back their livelihood, their lives.

When their priest saw us approach—we who represented church people back in the United States and Canada—he rushed up to us. "You gathered together your pennies from so many people and sent them to us," he said. "You were Jesus to us."

Church and Movement

The church is called to take an active role in fostering a movement for wholeness.

During the last century in the United States and Canada, throwing open the doors of the church and offering an extravagant welcome for whoever came through those doors represented best practice for a faithful, vital congregation. In the middle of the twentieth century people were looking for a church. Churches simply needed to be ready with a great offering of programs when discovered. Attraction was the name of the game.

But times have changed. We may build it, but they will not just come. Other activities have taken priority on Sunday and Wednesday nights, formerly the sacred time for church. Social norms no longer include weekly attendance at worship services. Churches cannot just open the doors and wait anymore. Those doors swing out, and we have to follow the arc of that swing. We have to exit the church building, going beyond the parking lot into all those unexpected places where Jesus might have gone—including on the road,[18] at the beach,[19] around the most unlikely people's supper tables.

It is not about attraction anymore; it is about action! The church needs to heed Jesus' advice. "Go!" says Jesus. Go into the entire world! Go! Make disciples!

All that "going" works best if it is strengthened by some equipping and some nurture. People cannot go forever without fuel. Churches continue to have a role as places of gathering in order to encourage the faithful, to equip people for going out, to prepare and train people for participation in a movement.

The church can serve as an oasis on the journey. It can function as a stopping place for rest and provisioning and refreshment for weary travelers. At the oasis, people check signals about what comes next. They learn new skills for the road ahead.

Churches can be places of training for action, like the churches involved in More Square working on labor justice in Kansas City, or the congregations in Indianapolis joining together in IndyCan to improve people's lives through better public transportation. They provide spiritual sustenance through worship, community life, study, and encouragement for spiritual disciplines.

The church, where we first experience the welcoming embrace of a loving God, where we learn to extend that love by loving neighbor and expanding the neighborhood to encompass the world, is also the place where we can train and provide for the journey into a twenty-first–century world of technological change and increasing diversity. It is the place where deep spirituality, true community, and a passion for justice converge into a hunger for wholeness in the spirit of Jesus' inauguration of the reign of God.

In eighth grade I heard a sermon I will never forget. From the pulpit came the words of a song from the radio. "What the World Needs Now Is Love, Sweet Love."[20] The preacher, Dr. Robert A. Thomas, represented anything but sentimentality. In a deep, gravelly, uncompromising voice he quoted the verse, and it took on more gravitas than when Burt Bacharach played it. In the midst of the Vietnam War, the Civil Rights Movement, and violence on our own college campuses, Dr. Thomas proclaimed, "What the world needs now is love," and I believed it. The message came not as sweetness but as searing, powerful light. It gripped me as a challenge worth a lifetime of pursuit.

Because we are loved, we can love. Every time we help put two broken pieces together, whether of communities or of individual lives, the number of fragments is fewer. Each one of us can choose to make our neighborhood and world a little better or a little worse. Eventually the droplets of our efforts join others to form a current. The words of the prophet Amos come to mind: "Let justice roll down like waters, / and righteousness like an ever-flowing stream."[21] A movement for wholeness rolls forward.

QUESTIONS

Chapter 4

1. When the world seems smaller than ever, why does the journey to remake the world seem longer? In your experience, is this the way it is?
2. What is different in the world today than it was in the world of your parents? How does this affect how we share God's love? Extend God's neighborhood of wholeness?
3. What existing world views need to change in order for churches or individuals or yourself to respond to the challenges of our time?
4. What can we learn from biblical examples such as Abram and Sarai and Moses leading the people through the desert at God's call?
5. How can churches function effectively in the wake of the changes that are taking place in the world today? In our twenty-first–century movement toward wholeness, what do we take with us from before? What do we leave behind? What do we invent that is new for this era?
6. What is your participation in the movement for wholeness?

5

Disciples of Christ
Who We Are

The door opened, letting laughter and warm air out into the New England winter. We passed the threshold quickly to join the "Shalom Meal" already underway. Our professor, Dr. Letty Russell[1] extended this hospitality each year as the fall semester moved to a close and Christmas drew near. Her students eagerly anticipated an evening of relaxation in the midst of final papers and exams.

Letty timed the annual event with Advent,[2] the Christian season that prepares us for the celebration of Jesus' birth. She had designed the Shalom Meal in part as a reminder that we can all start living now as if God's reign is already here. At the time of year when the Northern Hemisphere is literally the darkest, we gathered to eat and drink and laugh and engage in earnest conversation. We also worshiped God using words and songs that invited us to notice the signs of God's reign around us even now. In so doing, we readied ourselves to "rise" and "shine"[3] as bright lights in a dark season. We renewed our determination to live in justice, shalom, and wholeness, to live as if the world can already be whole—as God desires it to be.

Each Advent at Letty's house, we gathered at table. Toward the end of supper, we toasted signs of God's new era at the dawning of that New Year. To every instance named, we lifted a glass—to a mission trip completed, a sermon preached, a war concluded—to matters both weighty and small. We practiced noticing the evidence of God's reign among us; we named hints of wholeness…Shalom!

Signs of God's Reign

Attentive eyes catch glimpses of the reign of God already breaking into the world. Jesus' followers are called to be the primary signs. The church as part of a twenty-first–century movement for wholeness has the commission to be both evidence and training ground for God's shalom. Providing a witness to God's in-breaking reign is the church's quintessential mission.

A healthy church needs to offer: a community of welcome in the name of a God of love, an invitation to the communion table and to the table of true community, an understanding that God loves the world and desires that the world be whole and God's people be one, encouragement and equipping to join in expanding the circle of wholeness. Such signs of God's reign are what were found by the children at Oaktown, the twelve step members at Alamosa, the deported family members at Iglesia de Todas las Naciones in Tijuana, and the gay and lesbian persons at Central Christian in Indianapolis.

The church at its best offers to anyone who comes through the doors, either at their own initiation or because of Christian outreach, a sign of what Jesus talked about in his inaugural speech: bringing good news to the poor. It fosters the deep spirituality of the welcoming table, where people encounter the living God of love and are transformed into loving, welcoming persons themselves. At its best, the church helps extend a welcome into true community. It extends that community into an ever-expanding neighborhood where neighbors love and care for each other. The church participates with God in remaking the world and provides a platform from which to start living already into that transformation, proclaiming and living out of a passion for justice that includes all.

———

I read somewhere, and never forgot:

> "God did not tell the world to go to church,
>   but God did tell the church to go into the world!"

If daily life poses a mixture of delights and disappointments, meaningful work and boring routine that can be by turns exhilarating and exhausting, church offers periodic reprovisioning for the next phase of life's journey. That phase is, traditionally, "the next week." As mentioned in chapter 4, the congregation functions much like an oasis on a journey. Here people receive nurture and equipping to participate in a movement for wholeness.

At the oasis, worship provides spiritual reconnection with the living God who is the ultimate source of energy and hope and love. People learn to pray deeply, in order to draw upon God's power at all times. Community life offers support and challenge in appropriate measure, reinforcing the sense of belonging and care. Study opportunities help those at the oasis learn more about the ways of God for reconciliation, justice, and wholeness through shared Bible reading and reflection on God's action in the world today. Worship, prayer, community life, and study at the oasis all equip and provision the "traveler" for the journey ahead. In this sense, a person "goes to" church.

Church is also a place that a person "goes out from." Followers of Jesus pull into the oasis not only to be personally refreshed for our own private journey, but also to be reminded that we have a job to do for others. Having experienced God's welcome in the context of Christian community, each one now embarks on a new life of learning to extend that same welcome to others. Provisioning at church prepares us, individually and corporately, "to be and to share the good news" of God's love[4]: to show the world a better way to live as the walls of bitter divisiveness come tumbling down. Gathering with other followers of Christ on a regular basis reinforces the call to a way of love, which is part of God's larger movement to recreate the world into the place of wholeness that God originally intended. At the oasis, modern-day disciples equip themselves for the work at hand, forming part of a larger *movement*, which is a fitting way for church to function in the twenty-first century.

Churches sometimes live up to their promise both to nurture and send forth. Unfortunately, they do not *always* do so. Sometimes they lose connection with God's love and forget that God remains at the center of it all. Sometimes their cozy love for God and each other crowds out their attention to a hurting world. Sometimes community members come into conflict with each other and, instead of modeling an expansive community, become the prime example of divisiveness.

The church as part of a movement for wholeness experiences both wholeness and brokenness. Jesus also knew both.

In the World

Three times, Jesus had warned his disciples that the situation at Jerusalem would not be pretty.[5] Three times they had refused to hear it, even though, as they made their way toward the capital, the atmosphere grew palpably tense. Murmurings against Jesus in the highest places were getting louder. His talk of another kingdom already among them sounded like sedition to Caesar's officials. They would not tolerate it for long. Still Jesus kept on preaching. "The reign of God is among you," he said. He told story after story of what the kingdom was like.[6]

Meanwhile, the disciples' excitement was rising. If Jesus succeeded in inaugurating a new kingdom, which one of them would he select as his second in command? Jesus had to keep reminding them, "It won't be like that." In God's reign, the first will be last.

In the end, Jesus' warnings came to pass. He and the disciples came to Jerusalem, and indeed it was not pretty. Soldiers arrested Jesus on trumped up charges of sedition. The prosecutor gave him the opportunity to recant his claim that he, rather than Caesar, pointed toward God's realm. Jesus did not recant. Then came his brutal sentence. He was literally nailed to a couple of beams fashioned into a cross. The resulting slow and painful death took place in full public view. This Roman form of capital punishment functioned specifically as a warning to the population against insurrection. It was "state terrorism" in the truest sense of the term, and it had its intended effect. In the last horrific moments of Jesus' life, even his disciples fled and denied knowing him.

Surprisingly, in the next days, it just did not seem that he was dead. First came the issue of his missing body. It had disappeared from the burial tomb. A heavy boulder had blocked the entrance to the cave. Guards stood nearby, provided by the same empire that had killed him. And yet, Jesus' body had vanished without a trace.

Next, people kept seeing him alive, present in both body and spirit. He had a message for them: *Keep going forward. What I have told you is true. I am with you. God is with you. Life wins. Love triumphs. Go. Make disciples.*

Just over a month after his crucifixion came the Pentecost birth of the church. The Spirit of God danced and warmed the hearts of disciples. All of the people within earshot heard the gospel in their own languages, convicting them of their need for a kind of rebirth to a transformed way of life and binding them into new communities of love.

Finally, an even more surprising development occurred. One who had been their pursuer and persecutor met the living spirit of Jesus on the road and was transformed. Under his Greek name of "Paul," he started moving throughout the Mediterranean founding faith communities—churches—in the name of the God of love as known through the ministry, the death, and now the resurrection of Jesus.

Paul's journeys saw to it that the word spread. The church was established far and wide as he and others took seriously the instruction to "Go!"

These early followers of Jesus began to understand the resurrection as God's vindication of the life and message of Jesus. In particular, they interpreted it as proof of Jesus' conviction that "the kingdom of God is in your midst," immediately present with the lowest of the low, as well as the highest of the high. Jesus' resurrection confirmed for them that God intended to replace the division-based hierarchy of empire with an emerging new world guided by God-given rules of wide-open welcome. Jesus, though crucified, remarkably still moved in their midst. He stood as evidence of God's reign. He now passed on to them the calling to live as further testimony to God's reign of wholeness.

They sang and prayed their joy. Paul's letter to the Philippian church included probably the most glorious and well-known statement of the resurrection's powerful vindication of Jesus. Scholars think that Paul is quoting here from a hymn about Jesus that was already being sung in Christian communities.

> Let the same mind be in you that was in Christ Jesus,
>   who, though he was in the form of God,
>   did not regard equality with God
>   as something to be exploited,
>   but emptied himself,
>   taking the form of a slave,
>   being born in human likeness.
> And being found in human form,
>   he humbled himself
>   and became obedient to the point of death—
>   even death on a cross.
> Therefore God also highly exalted him
>   and gave him the name
>   that is above every name,
>   so that at the name of Jesus
>   every knee should bend,
>   in heaven and on earth and under the earth,
>   and every tongue should confess
>   that Jesus Christ is Lord,
>   to the glory of God the Father.[7]

Delivered in the context of an instruction to have "the same mind… that was in Christ Jesus," Paul presents the hymn as a powerful declaration of God's purpose in coming into the world in human form. John, the gospel writer, further explains this by describing Jesus as primary evidence of God's love for the world.[8]

A message was taking root about a God of love, a God of life and of new beginnings, a God of healing and wholeness. People did not just hear about it; they experienced it for themselves in communities of love and welcome that cut across social lines. They thought of themselves as followers of Jesus and took on the mantle of his embodied love as their personal charge.

People also started giving Jesus a new name: *Christ.*

—————

Jewish tradition had taught for generations about a "messiah" who would come to save the world. In Hebrew, "messiah" literally means "anointed one." In most cases in the Hebrew Bible, it refers to the Davidic king who sat on the throne in Jerusalem, who was anointed with ceremonial oil upon his election as king. In Babylonian exile in the mid-500s B.C.E., the anonymous prophet who gave us chapters 40—55 of the biblical book of Isaiah used the term "messiah" to refer to the Persian emperor Cyrus. This emperor had defeated the Babylonians and allowed Jewish exiles to return to Jerusalem and rebuild.[9] By the time of Jesus, many Jews thought that a messiah would rise up like David or Cyrus to free them from the Roman Empire. Some thought this savior would usher in a new age and rescue not only Israel but also the whole world.

As Jesus' reputation spread post-death and resurrection, as people began to experience God's love through a sense of Jesus' loving spirit still among them, his followers began to understand Jesus as the saving representative of God. The Greek word for messiah (transliterated into its English form) was *Christ.*

People began to experience the resurrected Jesus as the living Christ, the one who fully represented God's desire for a world made whole, starting with their own lives. They experienced his promise and presence as a liberating reality, freeing them from hopelessness and from fear of death. They remembered that he quoted a messianic scripture from Isaiah 61 at the beginning of his ministry:

> "The Spirit of the Lord is upon me,
> because he has anointed me
> to bring good news to the poor
> He has sent me to proclaim release to the captives..."[10]

They remembered his healing, his words of forgiveness, the communities restored. In all this they found a saving, liberating new reality. They began to call him Jesus the Messiah, or Jesus Christ. In the Syrian city of Antioch, the disciples of Jesus began to be called "Christians."[11]

Generic Disciples

In a certain cartoon, Jesus is depicted sitting under a tree in a beard and old-timey robes. He's looking like, well, like Jesus. A young person sits at his feet dressed in jeans and tee shirt. Jesus speaks. The caption reads, "No, not Twitter. Really. Follow me."

〰〰〰 〰〰〰 〰〰〰

Generically, the term "disciple" in a Christian context refers to any person who is a follower or student of Jesus Christ: a Christian. When Jesus of Nazareth gathered disciples, students of his teaching and example, they called themselves "followers of the way."[12] Though together on the path, these men and women[13] were individuals, each one with unique gifts and abilities and liabilities.

Then or now, Christians come in many varieties. Christians have in common the life, death, and resurrection of Jesus Christ teaching us to know God as a God of love. We see the many ways God is already transforming the world for justice and peace. We hear the call to represent God's love in the world. We catch a glimpse of who we can become at our best.

God's ways live among you, Jesus would say.[14] "The reign of God is at hand." Jesus' words and his way of life called followers to change the world's violent ways by living differently in it, as he had done. They became the first wave of God's reign by offering to each other the love that God has shown to humanity. When the missionaries in Nanjing chose to stay in solidarity with their Chinese colleagues and friends, they were living out the Christlike love of neighbor according to the rules of God's reign. They put flesh on the words of love—even at the risk of their own lives.

The church consists of Christ's disciples, people who seek to follow Jesus as he walked this life, remembering that he began his ministry by announcing good news to the poor, release to the captives, recovery of sight to the blind, and letting the oppressed go free. Disciples remember also that toward the end of his ministry Jesus made it clear: to properly serve Christ requires feeding the hungry people on our path, giving drink to the thirsty in our community, clothing the naked next to us. In fact, he said that in reaching out to such people we directly feed and clothe Christ himself. We represent a God who lives in the world through us and who calls upon us to join in the work of making this world a place where justice reigns, where peace prevails, and where all God's children are sheltered and fed and cherished.[15] We bring the promise of wholeness into existence by living it already.

Wholeness begins as we experience God's transforming love shown to us in communities that celebrate the life, death, and finally the resurrection of Christ. We respond by reaching out with the same kind of self-giving love for our neighbors. Little by little the world is changed.

⸺⟨⟨⟨⟩⟩⟩— ⸺⟨⟨⟨⟩⟩⟩— ⸺⟨⟨⟨⟩⟩⟩—

> He drew a circle that shut me out—
>   Heretic, rebel, a thing to flout.
> But Love and I had the wit to win:
>   We drew a circle that took him in!

Edwin Markham's poem[16] points out that having caught sight of God's intention for the world, people can respond in a variety of ways. We can start by trying to live already as though God's reign is indeed at hand. Or, realizing that all is not yet what it should be, we can barricade against the negative, making the walls ever higher between the world of danger and us.

In this book I have sought to describe a path that leads Jesus' disciples directly out into humanity to draw the circle larger. In a world that all too often cowers in fear, worries in isolation, sneers in cynicism—a world that believes the worst instead of working for the best—Christ's disciples strive to offer a community of faith whose hope is Spirit-breathed. The exuberant spirit of Pentecost still inspires prophets and saints and ordinary followers of Jesus today to run with patience the journey of faith, to live God's wholeness now.

We go rejoicing that God is love, and that God calls us to show that love by loving back. We go out into the neighborhood to expand it, just as Jesus came into the world himself in person. We go into the world with the resurrection assurance that, ultimately, life wins.

Resurrection Now

Not all Christians agree with my portrayal of God and the Christian faith. A loving God, known by the child's name "Daddy" (*Abba* in Jesus' language of Aramaic) is not the only picture of God that we see in the Bible.

The biblical creation narrative shows God providing a paradise of plenty.[17] The story also shows that God sends the first humans into a hard life of tilling the soil outside of paradise. Without human intervention, the earth is barren. Humans provide a necessary component. They help bring forth earth's plenty by going into the world rather than retreating into utopian purity. As humans move outside the secure walls, God continually reaches out to show divine care to humanity. Humanity does not always seem to comprehend, though, leaving God sometimes angry, even ready to call off the relationship. Repeatedly, however, God shows mercy and loving kindness. Humans may not be always be faithful to the relationship, but God is.

God's sustained displeasure comes when humans systematically mistreat each other. God consistently opposes all that would demean creation and diminish the fullness of life. This opposition often is described in scripture as God's anger; it is directed toward the privileged, yet uncompassionate, rich and powerful. The Bible's prophetic writings[18] show God completely frustrated with people who mistreat their workers or withhold help from the widow, the orphans, or the immigrant worker.

This angry picture of God can sometimes distract Christians from the main point, leading them to focus on the dividing lines between good and bad, between right and wrong, rather than on the wholeness that is our potential and God's desire. Rep. John Lewis has said, "Too many of us still believe our differences define us instead of the divine spark that runs through all of human creation."[19] Sadly, even Christians resist, or at least mistrust, the possibility for wholeness. They build barriers of condemnation instead of bridges of relationship. Central to the biblical tradition, however, is the view that God works by the power of steadfast love through attraction and persuasion rather than threats and punishment. Jesus is the supreme example.

In our world, powers-that-be do not easily give up power—as Jesus and his followers discovered. Even in our smaller ways, it is all too easy to live in contradiction to the promise of wholeness, to be compromised by our own timidity. And yet, Jesus after the cross shows that the risk we take by moving out into the world is worth it. Even following the Empire's cruel crucifixion, Jesus lives. The resurrected Christ demonstrates the faithfulness of God, who stays with humanity until the end. In Jesus Christ we see that God walks in solidarity with human beings. We learn that God's love is eternal. In Jesus' resurrection it all comes together.

━━◦⁄◦⁄◦⁊━━ ━◦⁄◦⁄◦⁊━ ━◦⁄◦⁄◦⁊━

We sat in the darkened theater. The movie also proceeded in darkened tones. The violence hardly let up. Never one to watch blood and gore, my experienced movie-eyes stayed shut for long sections of footage. But I couldn't shut my ears—not to the sounds of the beatings on the screen nor to the wailing of the child a few rows behind me whose parents had inexplicably brought him to see Mel Gibson's *The Passion of the Christ.*[20]

I had gone to the movie knowing what to expect: this extended focus on the brutality of Jesus' suffering and death. It is rightfully part of the story. A crucifixion was cruel.[21]

My genuine disappointment came at the conclusion of the story. At the end of the hours of suffering there appeared, for only a bare moment, a gleam of light suggesting…something. It did not last long enough or shine brightly enough to counteract or overcome what we had just experienced. It amounted to a slight nod at the power of life over death, a kind of ephemeral "resurrection lite." If you blinked, you might miss it.

I recommend instead a full-strength resurrection point of view.

The gut-wrenching truth is that a death is necessary for a resurrection to occur. Jesus offered himself up for that death. But his purpose is easily misunderstood. Jesus represents through both his life and his death the power of God with us. In Jesus' crucifixion we see something like what Captain James Lovell said of the moonshot Apollo 13: "Our mission was a failure but I like to think it was a successful failure."[22] In Jesus' death we see that God stays with us always. Even through death itself, God remains faithful. Life wins.

Though Jesus lived in a time of Roman oppression, he invited his disciples to act as if captivity had already given way to freedom, as if God had created a world of abundance with more than enough to go around. Jesus called his followers to extend mercy and kindness to others regardless of nation or clan, to be generous with their possessions and their community boundaries, to understand the world as belonging to God and to know God as a God of life and love who wants us to help make a difference in the world right now.

Christ's disciples today accept a mission to connect with the risen Christ among us, to become ambassadors for life as Jesus lived it. As Christ's emissaries we model the best of humanity rather than building barricades against the worst.

Jesus said the kingdom of God is among you, at hand. Resurrection begins as soon as we catch a glimpse of new life in God's love. Having first been loved, we want to share that love with others. We love in response to a loving God, not out of duty, nor even out of hope for eternal life. Eternal life has already begun in the moment of Christ's resurrection in us. We love out of a sheer response to a loving God who has created the universe good and whole and placed us, God's beloved, in the middle of it. We love because we are loved and so fulfill our calling to draw wider the circle of wholeness.

QUESTIONS

Chapter 5

1. What signs of God's in-breaking reign do you see in the world today? In what ways does your church participate as a sign of God's reign?

2. How in your experience is God a God of new beginnings?

3. What does "following Jesus as he lived his life" mean to you? What are some specific examples?

4. Where do you see the promise of wholeness compromised by your own timidity? By the timidity of the church?

5. What are some examples of when you or your church built bridges of wholeness rather than barriers of separation?

6

Christian Church
(Disciples of Christ)
Part of the One Body of Christ

Any Christian may be called a disciple of Christ. Yet in all this talk of wholeness, awkwardness arises for the denomination called the Christian Church (Disciples of Christ). We are Disciples of Christ, big "D," a separate and distinct group within the larger body of Christians. It is awkward because, in the beginning, we did not want to establish yet another division in the body of Christ. We still do not.

—————— —————— ——————

I am told that as the name of a church "Disciples of Christ" does not poll well; it sounds too much like the name for a cult. And yet, the Christian Church (Disciples of Christ) is an historic Protestant denomination along with United Methodists, Presbyterians, United Church of Christ, and others.

In fact, in my own lifetime, it has not been the exotic character of the name but its more generic ring that has proven problematic in describing Disciples.

—————— —————— ——————

When I was a child, a baby-sitter once asked me, "What church do you go to, anyway?" I answered, "The Christian Church," meaning the Christian Church (Disciples of Christ). She looked at me with exasperation. "Yeah. I know you're Christian. What kind of Christian?"

Of course she was frustrated. All those years ago, most people in North America assumed that everyone in the neighborhood was at least nominally Christian. They also assumed that Christianity was divided into a large number of parallel churches (denominations), each with a special twist to Christian identity.

In 2014, by contrast, in much of the United States and Canada people would not assume a person to be Christian at all. Their question might genuinely be, "What faith community do you belong to, if any?" And so the answer, "The Christian Church," in all its generic simplicity would be the best response in what would be a surprising topic for conversation in the first place!

—〰— —〰— —〰—

"We are Disciples of Christ…" So begins the identity statement of the Christian Church (Disciples of Christ). Or is it "disciples"— little "d"? Actually, it is both. As "little 'd'" disciples of Christ, we are followers of Christ like all other Christians. Well…not quite like all others. That is where the "big 'D'" comes in. When we refer to ourselves as a community distinct from other Christian denominations, we call ourselves Disciples, a shortened version of our longer name, the Christian Church (Disciples of Christ).

—〰— —〰— —〰—

Glasgow, Scotland, May 1809.[1] A young man walks into the church. He holds in his hand a "token," a little piece of metal given to him by the church elder. When Alexander produces that token at the communion table as evidence of his clergy-approved "worthiness," he will receive the bread and wine of communion.

On that particular day in 1809 Alexander Campbell did not eat the bread or drink from the cup. His growing sense that no human should bar another from the table of Christ overtook him. Rather than participate anymore in a system with which he could not agree, he laid down the token and walked away from the table. He became a proponent of communion open to all who followed Christ. He took the idea with him as he immigrated to America.

—◦◦◦◦◦— —◦◦◦◦◦— —◦◦◦◦◦—

The Christian Church (Disciples of Christ) first emerged on the American frontier in the early 1800s.[2] Its inspiration derived from the thinking of people like Alexander Campbell and his father, Thomas. At that time the "frontier" was located in what is now West Virginia and Kentucky.

As the settlers moved westward, "Disciples" (also known as "Christians") were among them. The generic sounding names of Disciples and Christians arose out of the hope that the divisions and barriers between "different kinds" of European Christians would become irrelevant in the "New World." People in the movement said of themselves, "We're not the only Christians but Christians only." They aspired to initiate a restored Christianity with room for everyone at the table of Christ.

In 1804, another of the movement's founders, a man named Barton W. Stone, participated with a group of pastors in dissolving their small, short-lived community. They explained their action in a document entitled "Last Will and Testament of the Springfield Presbytery," declaring, "We *will* that this body die, be dissolved, and sink into union with the Body of Christ at large."[3] Their action well represented the spirit of the time.

In the twenty-first century, Christians commonly ask why there should be denominations at all. Disciples have been asking this for two hundred years. Yet, in spite of ourselves, we have developed a unique culture of our own, with a certain way of being, with distinct practices, affinities, and shared memories. We now stand as a particular clan within the larger family of God in Jesus Christ. We still long, however, for the day when the unity of God's children will be apparent in a church without barriers of belief or practice.

—◦◦◦◦◦— —◦◦◦◦◦— —◦◦◦◦◦—

So, who are these "big D" Disciples?

Our historic desire to be "Christians only" has left us without a clear, broadly recognized definition. The "Design of the Christian Church (Disciples of Christ)" says, "[T]he Christian Church

(Disciples of Christ) is identifiable by its testimony, tradition, name, institutions, and relationships." Many have tried their hand at offering clarification.[4]

Rick Spleth, a regional church leader in Indiana, lists characteristics such as weekly communion, leadership of women and laity, an educated clergy, and the importance of scripture—as well as a priority on ecumenical life. [5] He rightly points out, however, that no one of these characteristics uniquely represents our community alone. We have a lot in common with other historic Protestants such as Methodists, United Church of Christ, Presbyterians, and Episcopalians. Bringing together a particular combination of beliefs and practices makes Disciples distinct. A twentieth-century Disciples video once said, "We baptize by immersion, so we're a bit like Baptists..." It went on to say that, in other ways, we also resemble Methodists, and in other ways Presbyterians.

Who are these Disciples of Christ? Let's take a closer look.

"Want to" People

A long-time Disciples leader in a rural congregation once told me, "Disciples are 'want to' people, not 'have to' people." In other words, Disciples pursue our faith freely, not out of a sense of duty or requirement. We follow Christ in grateful response to God's love, rather than out of fear of punishment. We're "want to" people.

The "want to" character of Disciples grows out of our historic focus on Christian unity, still a core value. We reject dogmatic formulas that serve to set a high bar on participation and to divide Christians from each other. We instinctively include whoever wants to be part, believing that God has already made us one in Christ. Unity for us is both "given" and "goal." It strikes us as a sad irony that Christianity, a religion about relationship and love, has all too often spawned divisiveness and bitter dispute. We maintain that the divisions within Christianity hinder the good news of a loving God who came into the world as Jesus to reconcile the world and make it whole. If people see unity among those of us who call ourselves Disciples (or disciples), they will more likely want to take part in God's project to heal the world. If someone "wants to" be part of the community, we rejoice.

—❦— —❦— —❦—

Jesus was in a town, teaching and healing. As usual, crowds surrounded him. By now people knew of his extraordinary healing presence, and they wanted to be near him. One particular woman had seen and heard. She had a long-standing medical condition that had left her penniless and a social outcast. Having seen what Jesus could do, she knew that if she could just get close and touch even the hem of his garment she might be healed. She worked her way through the crowds until she was able to stretch out her fingers to just barely graze the fringe of his prayer shawl. Sure enough, in that moment, she became well.[6]

The woman had known what would happen; she had already seen what he could do.

—❦— —❦— —❦—

Disciples of Christ have always thought that our actions, as followers of Christ, speak louder than our words. If, through the witness of Jesus, we know God to be a God of love and we are called to love each other, then how can we be divided against each other, especially violently divided?

People are watching.

Early Disciples of Christ believed that the message of God's love would be best shared with the world if Christians could first be seen to love each other. The divisions within the church needed to come to an end, they thought. That could happen if we would just get back to basics: deciding to follow Jesus, learning the stories of his ministry as told in the Bible, and living in his example of loving God and neighbor.

Those first Disciples worked hard to preach a simple gospel, eliminating denominational division from their practice. They participated in the great ecumenical worship feasts and camp meetings of the day. At these events people, regardless of denominational affiliation, worshiped together and proclaimed their love of God.[7]

Ever since then Disciples have tried to create worshiping communities free of doctrinal tests, so that whoever wants to can join in. The only requirement for formal affiliation is a public profession of faith in Jesus Christ, an affirmation that can take varied phraseology. The basic guide to life together is the Bible, especially the New Testament, as interpreted by both individual and community interacting with each other.[8]

For Disciples, communion is the central act of Christian worship. Given that in communion worshipers gather around Christ's table[9] at Christ's invitation, it has become the symbol of openness and unity. Disciples have come to believe that this table, where often the distinctions among Christians have been most rigidly enforced, needs instead to be an open table where all who want to follow Jesus are welcome.

No tokens necessary at the table of Christ.

All Means All

From the beginning, such radical welcome has meant that Disciples have experienced a great deal of diversity within our communities. This has been possible because Disciples (within the cultural limits of any particular era) have also stood passionately for the worth of each individual person. Individual worth is grounded in God's love for all, as Jesus demonstrated when he sat at table with social outcasts, "sinners," tax collectors, the sick, women, children— in a word: *anyone*. Jesus' followers are called to do likewise. All are welcome, and each individual is valued as a beloved child of God.

Valuing each individual was also originally consistent with the stated democratic values of the American frontier where Disciples first emerged. As Americans moved westward, they carried with them the resolve to be free and self-determining. Within the church, this meant that they declared freedom from hierarchy and from divisions created to mediate European disputes. In the young United States, early Disciples believed that each person could read his or her own Bible and prayerfully determine what it meant for his or her own life.

They touted biblical passages such as 1 Peter 2:9, which spoke to them of a "priesthood of all believers."[10] They believed that when congregations were established in newly settled towns, they could choose their own spiritual leaders by the same democratic principles being used in the political system. They could vote for their own leaders, often self-educated, who displayed spiritual maturity and biblical wisdom.

Today those values are still in evidence, although they have evolved as society and the church have changed. Disciples still hold passionately to the value of each individual person, and lift up the responsibility of each person to be accountable for his or her own spiritual journey. Part of that accountability includes involvement with a community of Christians who test against each other their own individual conclusions. We do not have extensive doctrine or a book of rules other than the Bible. As a result, different Disciples congregations take on different personalities. Some are liberal; some conservative; some reflect one or another ethnic group.

Within each congregation are individuals who have chosen to take part and who are making their own spiritual journeys in company with others. Through prayer and study of scripture and joint outreach to and with others, twenty-first–century Disciples seek to love the God who first loves us, and to show it by loving our neighbor as ourselves.

———

I first saw the frequently quoted saying that is attributed to St. Francis on a church sign board: "Preach the Gospel always; when necessary use words."

It seems a good reminder for Disciples of Christ.

———

Echoing through all of this is that Disciples like to keep it simple. We look to the example of Jesus as a model of God's love. All implications flow from there: the extravagant welcome, the impatience with divisive doctrine, and the radical valuing of each individual person within a larger context of wholeness. We often talk about our value for unity in diversity. Through the stories of Jesus that we read in the Bible, as well as our own experience in Christian community, we understand that God loves us, so we love God back and strive to show that love by loving God's other children, all God's children.

At our best, our love for Jesus is stronger to unite than anything else is to divide. Love brings us together; a love we learn from God through Jesus and from each other.

Cultivating Habits of Wholeness

In all truth, living united in the love of God *is* simple, but not easy. If Disciples or any other Christians were doing our job really well, that young woman who came to my office that day[11] would not have been so confused about Christianity, so vaguely frightened, in spite of her sense that something there could change her life for the better.

All too often, the image people have of Christianity is one of narrowness rather than inclusion, judgment rather than acceptance of different points of view, fear rather than love. The truth is that we Christians have a lot of work to do. We are not as good as we should be at showing the world what this God of love is like. We fall short of being the best possible ambassadors of that love.

We Disciples say that we want to be a church known for "true community, deep spirituality, and a passion for justice." The fact that Disciples often are not known at all says *we,* especially, have a lot of ground to cover.

—————

Part of the ground we have to cover is related to our context in a relatively new century. The twenty-first–century landscape, as we have already noted, is characterized by massive technological change, as well as generational and cultural diversity. The twentieth century saw the institutionalization of nineteenth-century movements of benevolence and mission. Six women drinking coffee and deciding to do something about homeless women and children led to a large ministry running dozens of benevolent institutions and sponsoring many more.[12] The model worked until the challenges of the twenty-first century called for something less corporate, more fluid. Now that same ministry, with fresh vision, fosters benevolence projects closer to the local congregation. Followers of Christ can again be empowered, as were the original six women, to be part of a renewed movement for wholeness.

The tree is large and expansive. Its leaves cover the branches heavy with fruit. But, surprise! The tree is upside down. Its bare roots reach up to the sky, while its branches, leaves, and especially the fruit touch the ground.

In this logo for the National Council of Spiritual Churches of Haiti,[13] the tree's roots extend upward to drink in nurture from God. It bears its fruit on the earth right now.

Jesus said that his disciples are known by their fruits.[14] The twenty-first–century church, as it approaches a new frontier of diversity and technological change, has the opportunity to help people bear and nurture the fruits of the spirit.[15] The whole argument of this book is predicated on the assumption that people meet the living Christ face to face even today, and bear those fruits starting now. Through the hospitality of the church, through the kindness and witness of Jesus' followers, people can catch a glimpse of the reign of God breaking in. They feel the welcome and want to be part of it and then become part of extending that welcome to others as well. For this circle to continue widening, churches need to brush up on habits of wholeness, including spirituality, community, and justice.

An article I once read said[16] that Christianity today is all too often merely a thin mixture of feeling good and doing good. This is not enough to sustain followers for the long haul. A real face-to-face engagement with a living God of love will give energy to fuel a long life of agape love and witnessing to God's wholeness. Disciples need to ask: Do people come into our congregations and feel God's presence?

Congregations further the movement for wholeness when they become centers of deep *spirituality*, places where Jesus demonstrably lives. Christian people need to be believable conduits of the present spirit of the living God. Every church that wants to go forward into the twenty-first century today can begin by asking: Do people here live as though God is alive and real in this place? A second question is: Do people sense true *community* here?

⁓⁓⁓   ⁓⁓⁓   ⁓⁓⁓

The "question and answer" session at the regional assembly of Disciples congregations had just finished. One of the questioners, predictably, asked about the church's stance on sexual orientation – an uncomfortable subject. In response, I had talked about Jesus' welcome at the table and our desire to emulate that welcome for all.

Now a young student stood before me. "Thank you," he said. "I'm in high school and I'm gay. At school I get bullied, but at church I feel safe and at home—just as you said."

As I shook his hand, I turned to greet another person in line—a middle-aged man. "I appreciate your words," he said. "I'm a conservative Republican. You made clear that I am welcome in my church as I am."

As we chatted, it turned out these two were from the same congregation. My words about table, welcome, and wholeness rang true because they experienced it already in the community of their congregation.

⁓⁓⁓   ⁓⁓⁓   ⁓⁓⁓

Twenty-first–century churches need to have strong habits of community that allow us to hold varied opinions about all manner of subjects, yet visibly stay together in love.

Disciples of Christ try to make this real through our understanding of the biblical notion of "covenant." This organizing metaphor in the "Design of the Christian Church (Disciples of Christ)" describes the structure and ministries of our denomination. Admittedly, our definition of the term is tempered by American democratic values of equality and freedom. We voluntarily agree to enter into a relationship with each other, and to be responsible to each other as we pursue a common mission. We enter into covenant with each other because God first entered into a covenant of love with us, as we see in the accounts of Noah, Abraham, David, Jeremiah, and others—including eventually Jesus.[17] In covenant, we join together freely, yet maintain accountability to each other for our joint witness and life.

I believe that three marks of covenant are particularly important for Disciples in the twenty-first century: civility in our dealings with each other, unity in our diversity, and shared commitment to mission beyond our walls. All of these are also marks of wholeness. The first, civility, calls us to tell the truth in love. It requires courageous but respectful conversations about difficult matters that threaten to divide.[18] Civility, courage, and mutual respect are also necessary for the second mark of covenant: unity in diversity.

———

Two Disciples pastors stood side by side before the crowd, looking solemn and a bit nervous. For a moment no one spoke. Then they began their stories. He served in a conservative, small-town setting. Her congregation had publicly announced their welcome of persons regardless of sexual orientation or identity.

The gathered assembly was about to vote on a question related to the region's policy on ordination and sexual orientation. These two were trying to set a tone of mutual respect for the debate that would follow.

They exchanged glances, seeming to take strength from each other. Then he fairly and accurately characterized her point of view. She respectfully and gently described his perspective. They acknowledged that they would not be voting the same way on the upcoming business item. Nevertheless, they were colleagues and friends, followers of Jesus, Disciples of Christ, and they would be at the table together after the vote, whichever way it went.

———

For Disciples, the challenge runs deeper even than making up our minds in faith on important issues. In times of deep divide, our witness is when we manage to remain together, staying in covenant, living out of our deeper unity in Christ—even with our difference of deeply held opinion. Holding onto each other, we become a sign of God's love, stronger to unite than opinions are to divide.

Disciples can and do disagree on many issues.[19] But we agree that Christ issues the invitation to the table in the church. Even with our different opinions, we share our love of God and our faith in Christ Jesus. We know there is much work we can do together concerning matters on which we *do* agree.

The challenge is real. If we are gay, we will not feel welcome in a church that may not allow us to serve. If we believe that same-sex orientation is contrary to the will of God, we will not feel completely comfortable in a church that ordains persons of different sexual orientations. Yet Disciples cherish the right and responsibility of individuals and congregations to take responsibility for personal or corporate faith journeys.[20]

We know that we will come to different conclusions. We do not lean on a council of church leaders, or a book of discipline, or even a general assembly to make the decision for us. Freedom of opinion within the constraints of love is part of what brings us to this community of faith in the first place. We love each other, though of different perspectives, because God first loved us. In many ways, this does not completely satisfy; however, it does provide an important witness in a society in which political disagreement leads to gridlock, and governments are blocked from moving forward even when we do agree.

<hr />

It has always been difficult to maintain this vision of community. Unity while honoring diversity is a challenge. Disciples, who were born in a desire to keep Christ's table open, have had trouble maintaining that openness ourselves.

Despite the open-table policy of Thomas Campbell and other early Disciples leaders, our church has struggled to understand who is to be invited and who should be denied. This has been true with regard to issues of race, women in leadership in the church, divorce and remarriage, and whether to accept the baptism of people from other Christian traditions.

The example and teaching of Paul the apostle helps us. He wrote primarily to offer counsel to congregations struggling with issues of inclusion and exclusion. Even he found it difficult to establish a consistent practice. On the one hand, his teaching about the role of women in the Corinthian church depended largely upon the social practices of his time and his desire that the church live peaceably in a tense political and social environment. On the other hand, he was aware of the deeper principles of the Christian faith, which he declared forthrightly in Galatians 3:28: "There is no longer Jew or Greek, there is no longer slave or free, there is no longer male and female; for all of you are one in Christ Jesus."

Unity does not mean uniformity. Quite the opposite. God's gift of unity is all the more precious when we disagree. It is what allows us to go forward to the third and most important mark of covenant.

The emphasis on shared mission beyond our walls—the third mark of covenant—grows out of God's own example of solidarity with the broken world. Taking human form, God is with us even to the point of death on a cross. Our covenant with each other is grounded in the covenant of healing, self-giving love that God made with the world in Jesus Christ. Our covenant with God and with one another calls us to equip ourselves to extend the neighborhood, reaching out to the world in love.

Love of neighbor means churches in the twenty-first century need to pursue our calling for *justice*: reaching out to others with an intention to see to it that our neighbor has access to the same things we want in life. Justice is at the core of a movement for wholeness. Jesus lives out there in the world. So should we. My husband, Rick Lowery, tells his ministry students, "If you want to see Jesus, go to Walmart and look into the faces of the people there." Rick's words remind students of Jesus' own admonition that he is visible in the faces of the "least of these," in all of us.

A Word for Disciples of Christ

I have often said that the Christian Church (Disciples of Christ) is a church whose time has come, and I believe it.

In a time of deep spiritual hunger, we strive to become ever more a church characterized by deep Christian spirituality. In an era of loneliness and alienation, we offer belonging in communities of faith and action. In a world of increasing globalization, we already share with long-established global partners a passion for inviting others into God's vision of justice and peace.

We are a church whose time has come. Our primary governance document, the "Design of the Christian Church (Disciples of Christ)," first adopted in 1968, envisioned one church in many places (congregations, regions, general ministries) connected by covenant, not hierarchy. Each ministry carries out its own mission according to God's particular call, but all share common values of oneness in Christ: an inclusive Lord's Table, a ministry of all believers, and a longing to live out God's vision of justice for all the earth.

Today, technology finally allows us to function in our various communities while remaining connected: missionaries in Congo e-mail stories to Indianapolis of a new orphanage, and, with a click of a computer key, those stories are spread around the church. We are many, but one: communities knit together by amazing, worldwide communication networks.

Many and diverse, but one: this has been our vision since the beginning. "Not the only Christians, but Christians only," still rings true. Today's world—diverse in culture, language, and creed, but increasingly one in economics, ecology, and information—stands in need of just such a vision. Our time has come.

My vision for Disciples is that we will continue to come into our own as a twenty-first-century church. Our community will grow in blessing and in depth as it necessarily grows more diverse. Our spirituality will find expression in lively worship that appeals to all senses, in prayer that involves our whole selves, in communities of hospitality and care. Our passion for justice will be fed by the increased diversity of our church as we begin to look more and more like the face of the world. Blessed by the energy of new, transformed, and diverse congregations and leaders, we will be a witness to reconciliation, a sacrament of wholeness for the whole human family.

Churches are important because they put flesh on the good intentions of the spirit. But more important than the specific church is the commitment to join with other followers in God's movement toward wholeness, to find the place where you can begin living as if God's reign is truly already breaking in among us. If you seek to take this journey among Disciples, know you are welcome. As a newcomer to a Disciples congregation in Arizona said, "'All means all' equals 'all means you.'"[21]

Setting Sail

For the Christian Church (Disciples of Christ), it is time again to move beyond the institutional form we adopted in the last century and head out into the world of the twenty-first century as a movement. We really do have to start living our desire for wholeness, like the bishops did in Constantine's time, and like the immigrants did in early North America.

The apostle Paul often described the church as a body, the body of Christ.[22] The image of one body made up of many parts well represents the unity-in-diversity basic to the church's nature. It provides one kind of metaphor for wholeness.

"Body" may be too functionally unified to work as an image for the Christian Church (Disciples of Christ), however. I see us as a fleet of boats, heading out onto the great sea of mission. Big boats, small boats, one-person crews, and many-handed ocean-liners, but all aligned around a common vision and mission, appropriately accountable to God and to each other in covenant, in ways that honor our individuality and that respect the distinctive missions of our various congregations and ministries. All the while, we acknowledge that we are one community in which what one does affects the other.

⸺⸺⸺

More importantly, how we act together reflects on the God we serve.

I sat on a panel of speakers: a psychologist, a historian, a couple of physics professors, and other representatives of religion. I spoke of a God of love.

"OK," said one of the others, "but what about the Crusades? For every act of Christian love you describe, I can tell you one of Christian hate." The other self-described atheists nodded in agreement.

It was tempting to point out that I would not hold the scientists responsible for Hiroshima or the psychologist to blame for every Freudian analysis ever gone awry. Still, it was a sobering moment.

People see in the actions of Jesus' followers something about the God we serve.

What are our churches "saying" to the world about wholeness and hope?

⸺ഽ൰ഽ⸺ ⸺ഽ൰ഽ⸺ ⸺ഽ൰ഽ⸺

Where next as we sail on into this century as Disciples of Christ?

Here is what I hope for us as we go forward: I hope that we will be steeped in our calling as disciples of Christ, that we will love God deeply and feel God's pain at the broken world, so different from God's intention made known in the reconciling life, death, and resurrection of Jesus. I hope that we will live out of our love for God and God's children, guided by a vision of shalom as described in the Torah and the prophets, by the joy of persons healed and communities restored as described in the stories of Jesus. I hope that we will be compelled by the words of Jesus' prayer in the gospel of John that we all be one and that we will therefore strive for wholeness, for unity, and for justice and peace.

I hope that our hearts will break over a a fragmented world and a divided church, and that we will call upon all communities of faith to witness to the wholeness that is already in the fabric of creation just waiting to be revealed in us. I hope we will challenge ourselves when our vision is too small, our horizon too close, or when we participate too fully in the isolation and individualism of our age. I hope we will care, cajole, challenge, and confront each other with the realities of our context and that we will respond to the call to seek justice, a nimble and mighty fleet on the move.

I hope that every time we gather around the table, when ordinary bread and juice become for us the presence of the living Christ, we will become again the body of Christ for the world, and we will remember and give thanks for the extraordinary power of life to win. I hope that we, as individuals and as church, will be a true sign and a welcoming invitation to the world to experience and participate in God's created wholeness.

Table 109

QUESTIONS

Chapter 6

1. Would people enter your congregation and feel the presence of the living God? Name some examples of how.

2. Are there controversial questions that your congregation finds difficult to discuss together? How does confidence in God's reconciling love help you stay together as a community of faith?

3. How does the concept of covenant help keep a balance between freedom and responsibility among Disciples?

4. What are ways that you or your congregation make real the love of God outside the walls of your home or church? What are you saying about wholeness and hope?

I

Preamble to the "Design of the Christian Church (Disciples of Christ)"

As members of the Christian Church,
    We confess that Jesus is the Christ,
    the Son of the living God,
    and proclaim him Lord and Savior of the world.
In Christ's name and by his grace
    we accept our mission of witness
    and service to all people.
We rejoice in God,
    maker of heaven and earth,
    and in God's covenant of love
    which binds us to God and to one another.
Through baptism into Christ
    we enter into newness of life
    and are made one with the whole people of God.
In the communion of the Holy Spirit
    we are joined together in discipleship
    and in obedience to Christ.
At the Table of the Lord
    we celebrate with thanksgiving
    the saving acts and presence of Christ.
Within the universal church
    we receive the gift of ministry
    and the light of scripture.

In the bonds of Christian faith
    we yield ourselves to God
    that we may serve the One
    whose kingdom has no end.
Blessing, glory, and honor
    be to God forever. Amen.[1]

II

Harmonies of Liberty

Isaiah 58:6–12; Matthew 22:6–40
Rev. Dr. Sharon E. Watkins
National Prayer Service; January 21, 2009

Mr. President and Mrs. Obama, Mr. Vice President and Dr. Biden, and your families, what an inaugural celebration you have hosted! Train ride, opening concert, service to neighbor, dancing till dawn...

And yesterday... With your inauguration, Mr. President, the flame of America's promise burns just a little brighter for every child of this land!

There is still a lot of work to do, and today the nation turns its full attention to that work. As we do, it is good that we pause to take a deep spiritual breath. It is good that we center for a moment.

What you are entering now, Mr. President and Mr. Vice President, will tend to draw you away from your ethical center. But we, the nation that you serve, need you to hold the ground of your deepest values, of our deepest values.

Beyond this moment of high hopes, we need you to stay focused on our shared hopes, so that we can continue to hope, too.

We will follow your lead.

There is a story attributed to Cherokee wisdom:

> One evening a grandfather was teaching his young grandson about the internal battle that each person faces.
>
> "There are two wolves struggling inside each of us," the old man said.
>
> "One wolf is vengefulness, anger, resentment, self-pity, fear...

"The other wolf is compassion, faithfulness, hope, truth, love…"

The grandson sat, thinking, then asked: "Which wolf wins, Grandfather?"

His grandfather replied, "The one you feed."

There are crises banging on the door right now, pawing at us, trying to draw us off our ethical center—crises that tempt us to feed the wolf of vengefulness and fear.

We need you, Mr. President, to hold your ground. We need you, leaders of this nation, to stay centered on the values that have guided us in the past; values that empowered us to move through the perils of earlier times, and can guide us now into a future of renewed promise.

We need you to feed the good wolf within you, to listen to the better angels of your nature, and by your example encourage us to do the same.

This is not a new word for a pastor to bring at such a moment. In the later chapters of Isaiah, in the 500s B.C.E., the prophet speaks to the people. Back in the capital city after long years of exile, their joy should be great, but things aren't working out just right. Their homecoming is more complicated than expected. Not everyone is watching their parade or dancing all night at their arrival.

They turn to God, "What's going on here? We pray and we fast, but you do not bless us. We're confused."

Through the prophet, God answers, what fast? You fast only to quarrel and fight and strike with the fist…

> Is not *this* the fast that *I* choose:
> to loose the bonds of injustice…
> …to share your bread with the hungry,
> and bring the homeless poor into your house?…
> Then your light shall break forth like the dawn,
> and your healing shall spring up quickly[2]…

At our time of new beginning, focused on renewing America's promise—yet at a time of great crisis—which fast do we choose? Which "wolf" do we feed? What of America's promise do we honor?

Recently Muslim scholars from around the world released a document, known as "A Common Word Between Us." It proposes a common basis for building a world at peace. That common basis?

Love of God and love of neighbor! What we just read in the Gospel of Matthew!

So how do we go about loving God? Well, according to Isaiah, summed up by Jesus, affirmed by a worldwide community of Muslim scholars and many others, it is by facing hard times with a generous spirit: by reaching out toward each other rather than turning our backs on each other. As Mahatma Gandhi once said, "People can be so poor that the only way they see God is in a piece of bread."

In the days immediately before us, there will be much to draw us away from the grand work of loving God and the hard work of loving neighbor. In crisis times, a basic instinct seeks to take us over—a fight/flight instinct that leans us toward the fearful wolf, orients us toward the self-interested fast...

In international hard times, our instinct is to fight—to pick up the sword, to seek out enemies, to build walls against the other—and why not? They just might be out to get us. We've got plenty of evidence to that effect. Someone has to keep watch and be ready to defend, and Mr. President—Tag! You're it!

But on the way to those tough decisions, which American promises will frame those decisions? Will you continue to reason from your ethical center, from the bedrock values of our best-shared hopes? Which wolf will you feed?

In financial hard times, our instinct is flight—to hunker down, to turn inward, to hoard what little we can get our hands on, to be fearful of others who may take the resources we need. In hard financial times, which fast do we choose? The fast that placates our hunkered-down soul—or the fast that reaches out to our sister and our brother?

In times such as these, we the people need you, the leaders of this nation, to be guided by the counsel that Isaiah gave so long ago: to work for the common good, for the public happiness, the well-being of the nation and the world, knowing that our individual well-being depends upon a world in which liberty and justice prevail.

This is the biblical way. It is also the American way—to believe in something bigger than ourselves, to reach out to neighbor to build communities of possibility, of liberty and justice for all. This is the center we can find again whenever we are pulled at and pawed at by the vengeful wolf, when we are tempted by the self-interested fast.

America's true character, the source of our national wisdom and strength, is rooted in a generous and hopeful spirit.

> "Give me your tired, your poor,
>   Your huddled masses yearning to breathe free,...
>   Send these, the homeless, tempest-tost to me..."[3]

Emma Lazarus' poetry is spelled out further by Dr. Martin Luther King Jr.: "As long as there is poverty in the world I can never be rich, even if I have a billion dollars. As long as diseases are rampant and millions of people in this world cannot expect to live more than twenty-eight or thirty years, I can never be totally healthy... I can never be what I ought to be until you are what you ought to be. This is the way our world is made."[4]

You yourself, Mr. President, have already added to this call: "If there's a child on the south side of Chicago who can't read, that matters to me, even if it's not my child... It's that fundamental belief—I am my brother's keeper, I am my sister's keeper—that makes this country work."

It is right that college classes on political oratory already study your words. You, as our President, will set the tone for us. You will help us as a nation choose again and again which wolf to feed, which fast to choose, to love God by loving our neighbor.

We will follow your lead—and we will walk with you. And sometimes we will swirl in front of you, pulling you along.

At times like these—hard times—we find out what we're made of. Is that blazing torch of liberty just for me? Or do we seek the "harmonies of liberty," many voices joined together, many hands offering to care for neighbors far and near?

Though tempted to withdraw the offer, surely Lady Liberty can still raise that golden torch of generosity to the world. Even in these financial hard times, these times of international challenge, the words of Katherine Lee Bates describe a nation with more than enough to share: "Oh, beautiful for spacious skies, for amber waves of grain, for purple mountain majesties above the fruited plain..."

A land of abundance guided by a God of abundance, generosity, and hope—this is our heritage. This is America's promise, which we fulfill when we reach out to each other.

Even in these hard times, rich or poor, we can reach out to our neighbor, including our global neighbor, in generous hospitality, building together communities of possibility and of hope. Even in these tough times, we can feed the good wolf, listen to the better angels of our nature. We can choose the fast of God's desiring.

Even now in these hard times let us:

> Lift every voice and sing
> Till earth and heaven ring,
> > ...with the harmonies of Liberty;

Even now let us sing a song full of hope...

Especially now, from the center of our deepest shared values, let us pray, still in the words of James Weldon Johnson:

> Thou who has by Thy might
> > Led us into the light,
> > Keep us...in the path, we pray.
> > Lest our feet stray from the places, our God, where we
> > met Thee,
> > Lest, our hearts drunk with the wine of the world, we
> > forget Thee;
> > Shadowed beneath Thy hand,
> > May we forever stand.
> > True to our God,
> > True to our native land.[5]

III

Principles Of Identity—
as articulated by the
21ˢᵗ Century Vision Team

1. We confess that Jesus is the Christ, the Son of the Living God, and proclaim him Lord and Savior of the world, requiring nothing more—and nothing less—as a basis of our life together.
2. We hold the centrality of scripture, recognizing that each person has the freedom—and the responsibility—to study God's Word within the community of the church.
3. We practice the baptism of believers, which emphasizes that God's grace demands a response of faith and discipleship, while also recognizing the baptism performed in other churches.
4. We gather for the Lord's Supper, as often as possible, experiencing at this table the gracious, forgiving presence of Jesus Christ.
5. We structure our community around the biblical idea of covenant, emphasizing not obedience to human authority but accountability to one another because of our shared obedience to Christ.
6. We participate in God's mission for the world, working with partners to heal the brokenness of creation and bring justice and peace to the whole human family.
7. We hear a special calling to make visible the unity of all Christians, proclaiming that in our diversity we belong to one another because we commonly belong to Christ.

8. We witness to the Gospel of God's saving love for the world in Jesus Christ, while continuing to struggle with how God's love may be known to others in different ways.

9. We affirm the priesthood of all believers, rejoicing in the gifts of the Holy Spirit—which include the gift of leadership—that God has given for the common good.

10. We celebrate the diversity of our common life, affirming our different histories, styles of worship, and forms of service.

11. We give thanks that each congregation, where Christ is present through faith, is truly the church, affirming as well that God's church and God's mission stretch from our doorsteps to the ends of the earth.

12. We anticipate God's coming reign, seeking to serve the God— Creator, Redeemer, and Sustainer—whose loving dominion has no end.

IV

Five Covenantal Values
of the Christian Church
(Disciples of Christ)

as articulated by William Chris Hobgood,
General Minister and President of the
Christian Church (Disciples of Christ)
2003–2005

1. We believe that Jesus is the Christ, the Son of the living God, and
   we accept him as our Lord and Savior. (Matt. 16:16)
2. We believe the Lord's Supper to be an open and inclusive call to
   radical hospitality. (1 Cor. 11:28)
3. We affirm the ministry of the priesthood of all believers: i.e., by
   our baptism we are all ministers.
4. The love of unity, wherein we are called to lead in the healing of
   a broken church and a broken world, has always been a passion
   for those of us called Disciples of Christ. (John 17:21)
5. A passionate commitment to creating a just and human world is
   the kind of ethics that grows out of our love for God and God's
   love for us and the whole world.

William Chris Hobgood. *Born Apart, Becoming One: Disciples
Defeating Racism* (St. Louis: Chalice Press, 2009).

Notes

Introduction

1 Those who served on the 21ˢᵗ Century Vision Team (with their employment/ designation at the time): **Diana Batzka**, Seminarian, Vanderbilt Divinity School, Nashville, Tenn.; **Adonna Bowman**, Executive Director, Office of Disciples Women, Disciples Home Missions, Indianapolis, Ind.; **David Brown**, Member, Lindenwood Christian Church, Memphis, Tenn.; **Charlie Gaines**, Former Second Vice-Moderator, and member, First Christian Church, Arlington, Texas; **Brian Gerard**, Pastor, First Christian Church, Louisville, Ky.; **Cynthia Hale**, Pastor, Ray of Hope Christian Church, Decatur, Ga.; **Carolyn Ho**, Former First Vice Moderator, and member, Queen Anne Christian Church, Seattle, Wash. (currently living in Russia); **Verity Jones**, Publisher and Editor, *DisciplesWorld* Magazine, Indianapolis, Ind.; **Sara LaRoche**, Seminarian, Christian Theological Seminary, Indianapolis, Ind.; **William Lee**, Pastor, Loudon Avenue Christian Church, Roanoke, Va.; **Michael Kinnamon**, General Secretary, National Council of Churches, New York, N.Y.; **Steve Mason**, Seminarian, Vanderbilt Divinity School, Nashville, Tenn.; **Shauna McGhee**, Pastor, Vision Christian Church, Lexington, Ky.; **Tamara Rodenberg**, Dean, Disciples Seminary Foundation, Claremont, Calif.; **Juan Rodriquez**, Pastor, Iglesia Del Pueblo–Hope Center Christian Church, Hammond, Ind.; **Sharon E. Watkins**, General Minister and President, Christian Church (Disciples of Christ), Indianapolis, Ind.; **Wanda Bryant Wills**, Executive Director/Communications, Office of General Minister and President, Indianapolis, Ind.; **Johnny Wray**, Director, Week of Compassion, Indianapolis, Ind.

2 General Minister and President of the Christian Church (Disciples of Christ) from 1993–2003. Author of *2020 Vision for the Christian Church (Disciples of Christ)* (St. Louis: Chalice Press, 2001)

3 For a statement that is often used as an "affirmation of faith" by Disciples, please see appendix 1: Preamble to the "Design of the Christian Church (Disciples of Christ)."

Chapter 1: Table

1 Mary Roach, *Packing for Mars: The Curious Science of Life in the Void* (New York; London: W.W. Norton & Company, 2010), 271.

2 Jon Meacham, "The End of Christian America," April 3, 2009, www.newsweek. com/2009/04/03/the-end-of-christian-america.html.

3 Todd M. Johnson, Ph.D., "Christianity in Global Context: Trends and Statistics," http://www.pewforum.org/files/2013/04/051805-global-christianity.pdf.

4 "'Nones' on the Rise," PewResearch Religion & Public Life Project, October 9, 2012, http://www.pewforum.org/2012/10/09/nones-on-the-rise/.

5 Luke 19:1–10.

6 Matthew 9:10–13; Luke 15:2

7 John 4:1–42.

8 Matthew 19:14; Mark 10:14; Luke 18:16.

9 Luke 6:15.

10 Twelve Step Groups are involved in programs designed to help individuals overcome addictions or traumatic experiences by following twelve principles in a progression toward recovery. The most well-known twelve step program is Alcoholics Anonymous.

11 ἀγάπη, Henry George Liddell, Robert Scott, "A Greek-English Lexicon," on Perseus via Wikipedia, "Greek words for love."

12 Luke 10:29–37.

13 Luke 4:17–19; cf. Isaiah 61:1–2.

14 Isaiah 1:10–17; 58:1–14; Amos 5:11–24; Micah 6:6–8; see also Deuteronomy 14:28–29; 15:7–11.

15 Genesis 18:1–16.

16 Genesis 37—50 and Exodus 1—15.

17 Exodus 16.

18 Luke 15:11–32 (the parable of the prodigal son).

19 Deuteronomy 6:5.

20 Matthew 22:35–40; Mark 12:28–31; Luke 10:25–28; Leviticus 19:18.

21 The Christian Church (Disciples of Christ) in the United States and Canada, www.disciples.org.

22 John 13:2b–20, 34–35.

23 Thanks to the Reverend Julie Richardson Brown for this story, via the Reverend John Richardson.

24 "Jesus Loves Me." Words: Anna Bartlett Warner, 1860. Music: William Batchelder Bradbury, 1862.

25 *Places in the Heart.* Director: Robert Benton. Cast: Sally Field, Lindsay Crouse, Ed Harris, Amy Madigan, John Malkovich, Danny Glover, and Terry O'Quinn. Delphi II Productions and TriStar Pictures, 1984. Film.

Chapter 2: Welcome

1 *Portrait of Ireland,* Lisa Gerard-Sharp and Tim Perry, main contributors (London: Dorling Kindersley Limited, 2000), 196–97.

2 The original idea was created by the Reverend Jon Goeringer and implemented at First Christian Church, Elk City, Oklahoma. Called "Good News Dinners," the

National Evangelistic Association, Lubbock, Texas, promoted the idea among their many program offerings.

3 John 4:1-42.

3 From www.habitat.org, Habitat's credo: "Habitat for Humanity believes that every man, woman and child should have a decent, safe, and affordable place to live. We build and repair houses all over the world using volunteer labor and donations. Our partner families purchase these houses through no-profit, no-interest mortgage loans or innovative financing methods."

5 From www.humaneborders.org, their credo: "Humane Borders, motivated by faith, offers humanitarian assistance to those in need through the deployment of emergency water stations on routes known to be used by migrants coming north through our desert."

6 Jolin Wilks McElroy, Pastor, church newsletter article. First Christian Church, Charlotte, North Carolina. December 2008.

7 Matthew 14:13–21; Mark 6:30–44; Luke 9:10–17; John 6:5–14. While many of the stories about Jesus are told more than once in the Bible, this story, "The Feeding of the 5000," is one of the rare ones to be told four times, once by each of the gospel writers.

8 (The play on words actually works better in French. "Il ne s'agit pas seulement du salut de l'ame; mais egalement du salut de l'homme.") These words of Rev. Jean Bokeleale, ca. 1978, have a resonance with James 2:14–18.

9 See chapter 1 for original discussion of this story.

10 For more on the original intention of the "Homogeneous Unit Principle," please go to www.lausanne.org/en/documents/lops/71-lop-1.html.

11 Luke 4:25–27.

12 Genesis 18:1–8.

13 1 Kings 17:8–24; 2 Kings 5:1–19.

14 Rev. Jorge Cotto in an e-mail to Sharon Watkins, August 28, 2013.

15 Personal visit to Oaktown, Indiana, 2011.

16 Personal visit, September 2012.

17 Diana Butler Bass, *Christianity After Religion: The End of Church and the Birth of a New Spiritual Awakening* (New York: HarperOne, 2012).

18 Democratic Republic of Congo, then known as the Republic of Zaire.

19 Millard Fuller, *Bokotola* (New York: Association Press, 1977), 156.

Chapter 3: Wholeness

1 John 17:20–21.

2 Apartheid, *noun* : racial segregation; *specifically*: a former policy of segregation and political and economic discrimination against non-European groups in the Republic of South Africa. "Apartheid." *Merriam-Webster.com*. Merriam-Webster, n.d. 4 Jan. 2014. www.merriamwebster.com/dictionary/apartheid

3 Peter Storey, "Remembering the Ecumenical Struggle against Apartheid," *Word & World*, vol. 18, no. 2 (Spring 1998):

4 Ibid.

5 "WCC Honours the Legacy of Mandela," 06 December 2013. http://www. oikoumene.org/en/press-centre/news/wcc-honours-the-legacy-of-mandela.

6 Matthew 28:19.

7 "Meet Helen and David Popp," *The Place 2B Newsletter* (January 2013), http:// theplace2b.org/2012/01/meet-helen-and-david-popp/.

8 Isaiah 9:7.

9 Isaiah 11:6.

10 Psalm 85:10–11.

11 For a more extensive discussion of *shalom,* please see *The Brown-Driver-Briggs Hebrew and English Lexicon* (1906, repr., Peabody, Mass.; Hendrickson, 1996).

12 Revelation 21:24.

13 Genesis 1—3.

14 Isaiah 61:1–2.

15 For a more extensive discussion of this, see Peter Brown, *Poverty and Leadership in the Later Roman Empire* (Waltham, Mass.: Brandeis, 2001).

16 Emperor Theodosius, in 380, declared the Catholic Church as the only legitimate imperial religion.

17 Paraphrase of Acts 14:16-17.

18 Elizabeth Pond, "The Berlin Wall: What Really Made It Fall," *The Christian Science Monitor,* October 8, 2009, http://www.csmonitor.com/Commentary/ Opinion/2009/1008/p09s05-coop.html?cmpid=addthis_email#.Ufu2Bz2r4Yc. email.

19 As told to Rick Lowery.

20 Pond, "The Berlin Wall."

21 ἡ βασιλεία τοῦ θεοῦ, in the original Greek, is usually translated "kingdom of God" in English Bibles; however, its meaning is broader than a physical kingdom, and encompasses the people and the lives they are called to live within the reach of God's reign.

22 Matthew 5:1–12, "The Beatitudes."

23 Matthew 5; Mark 9:50.

24 Matthew 4:17, Mark 1:15; Luke 17:21.

25 Matthew 13:31–32; Mark 4:31; Luke 13:18–19.

26 Matthew 13:33; Luke 13:20–21.

27 Matthew 25:31–40.

28 John 15:12–13.

29 Matthew 28:19a.

30 Matthew 14:16; Luke 9:13; Mark 6:37.

31 As told to Todd Adams, Associate General Minister and Vice President, by Howard Dentler, former Deputy General Minister and Vice President, ca. 2012. At this time Fiers would have been the executive secretary for the International Convention of the Christian Churches (Disciples of Christ).

32 Editorial, *Washington Post,* February 13, 2014.

33 Micah 6:8.

34 Community, Country Club, St. Andrew, and Swope Parkway United.

35 Luke 4:18a.

36 Micah 6:8.

37 In Donald B. Ardell, *High Level Wellness* (Emmaus, Pa.,: Rodale, 1977). Available online at http://www.seekwellness.com/wellness/upstream-downstream.htm.

38 See chapter 2 treatment of Genesis 18:1–15.

39 Bob Marley, *"Them Belly Full (but We Hungry)."* Island/Tuff Gong. 1974. Album.

40 Martin Luther King Jr. Montgomery, Alabama. March 25, 1965. Speech.

41 Revelation 22:2.

Chapter 4: Movement

1 Iris Chang, *The Rape of Nanking: The Forgotten Holocaust of World War II* (New York: Basic Books, 1997), 129–39.

2 Then it was called "short term missionary." Like the GMIs of today, the program was administered by Disciples Division of Overseas Ministries and funded by Week of Compassion.

3 2013 World Hunger and Poverty Facts and Statistics, World Hunger Education Service. http://www.worldhunger.org/articles/Learn/world%20hunger%20facts%202002.htm.

4 Susan Heavey, "U.S. Poverty Rate Remains High even Counting Government Aid," *Reuters,* November 6, 2013.

5 Dodd-Frank Wall Street Reform and Consumer Protection Act. Pub. L. 111-203. 124 Stat. 1376-2223. 21 Jul 2010. Comprehensive summary of it is available at http://www.banking.senate.gov/public/_files/070110_Dodd_Frank_Wall_Street_Reform_comprehensive_summary_Final.pdf.

6 For more on the Democratic Republic of Congo, please see http://www.friendsofthecongo.org/news.html and www.globalministries.org.

7 Thomas Friedman, *The World Is Flat: A Brief History of the Twenty-First Century* (New York: Farrar, Straus and Giroux, 2005).

8 Reza Aslan, *No god but God: The Origins, Evolution, and Future of Islam* (New York: Random House, 2006).

9 For more information on this ministry today, please see http://www.nbacares.org/.

10 Genesis 12:1–4.

11 From http://www.pewsocialtrends.org/2012/05/17/explaining-why-minority-births-now-outnumber-white-births/ .

12 Phyllis Tickle, *The Great Emergence: How Christianity Is Changing and Why* (Grand Rapids, Mich.: Baker Books, 2008).

13 Exodus 1—15.

14 Genesis 50:25; Joshua 24:32.

15 Exodus 33:3.

16 This analysis of how the movement took shape draws heavily on: Charles Duhigg, *The Power of Habit: Why We Do What We Do in Life and in Business* (New York: Random House, 2012).

17 Loren Eiseley, "The Star Thrower," *The Unexpected Universe* (New York: Harcourt, Brace &World, 1969).

18 Luke 24:13–35.

19 John 21:4–19.

20 "What the World Needs Now Is Love." Words: Hal David. Melody: Burt Bacharach. 1965.

21 Amos 5:24.

Chapter 5: Disciples of Christ

1 Letty M. Russell, *Church in the Round: Feminist Interpretation of the Church* (Louisville: Westminster John Knox Press, 1993); *idem, Human Liberation in a Feminist Perspective: A Theology* (Louisville: Westminster John Knox Press, 1974); *idem, Just Hospitality* (Louisville: Westminster John Knox Press, 2010).

2 Advent is the first season of the Christian liturgical year. Four Sundays before Christmas, the scripture readings, prayers, and hymns form a month of preparation for Christmas by focusing attention on the conviction that God is at work to heal and transform the broken and unjust world of our experience into "the kingdom or reign of God," where justice, peace, and love prevail. The themes of Advent include both an honest, often searing prophetic judgment against the injustices and dysfunctions of the world and a hopeful celebration of the new world God is creating. As the Sundays move toward Christmas, the scripture readings, particularly the gospels, move toward the birth of Jesus. Biblical themes of light shining in darkness are visually represented by the lighting of candles, one for each of the four Sundays of Advent, culminating in the lighting of a fifth candle at the center, the "Christ candle" that is lighted at the Christmas service, traditionally at midnight, as Christmas Eve turns to Christmas Day.

3 The Advent scriptures from the Hebrew Bible and the gospels in the Revised Common Lectionary, which is the three-year cycle of readings typically used by Disciples and other "mainline Protestant" denominations are as follow: Isaiah 2:1–5; 11:1-10; 35:1–10; 7:10–16; 64:1–9; 40:1–11; 61:1–4, 8–11; 2 Samuel 7:1–11, 16; Jeremiah 33:14–16; Malachi 3:1–4; Zephaniah 3:14–20; Micah 5:2–5a; Matthew 24:36–44; 3:1–12; 11:2–11; 1:18–25; Mark 13:24–37; 1:1–18; John 1:6–8, 19–28; Luke 1:26–38; 21:25–36; 3:1–6; 3:7–18; 1:39–45.

4 From the Christian Church (Disciples of Christ) mission statement adopted in 2001: "Our mission is to be and to share the Good News of Jesus Christ, witnessing, loving, and serving, from our doorsteps to the ends of the earth."

5 Mark 8:31–33; 9:30–32; 10:32–34. See also Matthew 16:21–28; 20:17–19; Luke 9:22–27, 18:31–34.

6 See especially Matthew 13, and parallels found in Mark and Luke. Also, John 3.

7 Philippians 2:5–11.

8 John 3:16–17.

9 Isaiah 45:1.

10 Luke 4:18, quoting part of Isaiah 61:1.

11 Acts 11:26.

12 Acts 9:2; 11:26; 19:23; 22:4; 24:14, 22.

13 Though the Twelve Disciples were all men, several women were known to have been part of Jesus' following as well. See Luke 8:1–3, for example.

14 Matthew 4:17 and 10:7; Mark 1:14–15; Luke 17:21.

15 This concern for those on the margins of society is often referred to as "God's preferential option for the poor." Although derived from scripture (especially Matthew 25:31-46), the phrase was first defined in detail by Gustavo Gutierrez in his landmark *A Theology of Liberation* (Lima: CEP, 1971).

16 Edwin Markham, "Outwitted." Disciples poet (1852–1940).

17 For a full treatment of a theology of abundance related to Sabbath wholeness, see Richard H. Lowery, *Sabbath and Jubilee* (St. Louis: Chalice Press, 2000). For a comprehensive treatment of the early Church's focus on "present paradise" and the "beautiful feast of life," see Rita Nakashima Brock and Rebecca Ann Parker, *Saving Paradise* (Boston: Beacon Press, 2008).

18 See, for example: Isaiah 58; Amos 5:21–24; Micah 6:6–8.

19 Rep. John Lewis's remarks on the 50th Anniversary of the March on Washington, August 28, 2013.

20 *The Passion of the Christ*. Director: Mel Gibson. Writers: Benedict Fitzgerald, Mel Gibson (screenplay). 2004. Film.

21 For an interesting and helpful discussion of the possible meanings of the violence of the crucifixion please see. Clark M. Williamson, "Atonement Theology and the Cross," *Encounter* 71 (2010): 1–25. Williamson says: "…there are two views of God that run like parallel railroad tracks throughout the Bible, from early in the scriptures through to the end. One is the God of nonviolence; the other is the God of violence… Consequently there are two versions in the Bible of how everything will end up: either in a Final War or in a Final Banquet… God is the God of a singular promise and a singular command. The promise is that we are to understand ourselves as unconditionally loved by God; the command is that in response we are to love God with all our selves and our neighbors as ourselves."

22 James A. Lovell, (1975) in, "'Houston, We've Had a Problem,'" in Edgar M. Cortright, *Apollo Expeditions to the Moon*. Washington, D.C.: NASA. NASA SP-350. Retrieved July 4, 2013. "Survive we did, but it was close. Our mission was a failure but I like to think it was a successful failure." Chapter 13.1 - http:// history.nasa.gov/SP-350/ch-13-1.html – retrieved September 1, 2013

Chapter 6: Christian Church (Disciples of Christ)

1 Disciples of Christ Historical Society webpage. http://www.discipleshistory.org/ online/artifact/archives/spring_2010.htm

2 There are many good treatments of Disciples history, including those footnoted throughout this book. For a helpful view of some the diverse currents that make up this stream see Sandhya Jha, *Room at the Table. Struggle for Unity and Equality in Disciples History* (St. Louis: Chalice Press, 2009).

3   *The Encyclopedia of the Stone-Campbell Movement,* edited by Douglas A. Foster, et al (Grand Rapids: Eerdmans, 2004), 453–55.

4   Please see appendices 3 and 4 for two such descriptions that I find helpful.

5   See http://indianadisciples.org/about/basic-beliefs/.

6   Matthew 9:20–22; Mark 5:25–34; Luke 8:43–48.

7   Mark G. Toulouse, *Joined in Discipleship: The Maturing of an American Religious Movement* (St. Louis: Chalice Press, 1992), 26.

8   A good guide to how Disciples study the Bible can be found in M. Eugene Boring, *Disciples and the Bible: A History of Disciples Biblical Interpretation in North America* (St. Louis: Chalice Press, 1997).

9   Communion is traditionally and formally called Eucharist, from the Greek word for "thanksgiving." For more extensive treatment of Disciples understanding of communion in an ecumenical context, see Keith Watkins, *The Great Thanksgiving: The Eucharistic Norm of Christian Worship* (St. Louis: Chalice Press, 1995).

10   The exact quote is: "But you are a chosen race, a royal priesthood, a holy nation, God's own people…"

11   See chapter 1.

12   See chapter 4.

13   For more information on our Disciples partners CONESPEH, see www.globalministries.org.

14   Matthew 7:15–20; "[Y]ou will know them by their fruits" (v. 20).

15   In Galatians 5:22–23, Paul talks about "the fruit of the Spirit": love, joy, peace, patience, kindness, generosity, faithfulness, gentleness, and self-control.

16   See John Blake, "Author: More Teens Becoming 'Fake' Christians." http://www.cnn.com/2010/LIVING/08/27/almost.christian/, which is a discussion of Kenda Creasy Dean, *Almost Christian: What the Faith of Our Teenagers Is Telling the American Church* (Oxford: Oxford University Press, 2010).

17   Genesis 9:9–17; 15:1–21; 17:1–27; 2 Samuel 7; Jeremiah 31:30–33; 32:36–44; 1 Corinthians 11:23–26.

18   For more on courageous conversations, see Ronald A. Heifetz, Marty Linsky, and Alexander Grashow, *The Practice of Adaptive Leadership: Tools and Tactics for Changing Your Organization and the World* (Boston: Harvard Business Press, 2009).

19   For resources to help congregations hold conversations about difficult and controversial issues, please see: William Paulsell, ed., *Listening to the Spirit: a Handbook for Discernment* (St. Louis: Christian Board of Publication, 2001); also see "Talking Together as Christians About Tough Social Issues," Evangelical Lutheran Church in America, Division for Church in Society, and "Moral Discernment in the Churches. A Study Document" (1999); and "Faith and Order Paper No. 215," (World Council of Churches Publications, 2013).

20   Traditional Disciples language would be: to rightly discern the word of truth.

21   As told to me by the Rev. Dale Suggs, interim pastor at Foothills Christian Church, Glendale, Arizona.

22   Romans 12:4–5; 1 Corinthians 12:12–31.

Appendices

1 See www.disciples.org.

2 Isaiah 48:6–8, emphasis added.

3 Emma Lazarus, "The New Colossus," 1883.

4 As quoted in *The Words of Martin Luther King, Jr.,* selected by Coretta Scott King (New York: Newmarket Press, 1983), 21.

5 James Weldon Johnson, "Lift Every Voice and Sing," 1900.